The Constitution of
The State of Colorado
A Quick Reference Guide

Bootblack Budget Books
Copyright 2018 ©
ISBN-13: 978-1985767423
ISBN-10: 1985767422

Contents:

Preamble – Page 39

Article I: Boundaries – Page 40

Section 1. Boundaries

Article II: Bill of Rights – Page 41

Section 1. Vestment of Political Power

Section 2. People May Alter or Abolish Form of Government Proviso.

Section 3. Inalienable Rights

Section 4. Religious Freedom

Section 5. Freedom of Elections

Section 6. Equality of Justice

Section 7. Security of Person and Property Searches Seizures Warrants

Section 8. Prosecutions Indictment or Information

Section 9. Treason Estates of Suicides

Section 10. Freedom of Speech and Press

Section 11. Ex Post Facto Laws

Section 12. No Imprisonment for Debt

Section 13. Right to Bear Arms

Section 14. Taking Private Property for Private Use

Section 15. Taking Property for Public Use Compensation, How Ascertained

Section 16. Criminal Prosecutions Rights of Defendant

Section 16a. Rights of Crime Victims

Section 17. Imprisonment of Witnesses Depositions Form

Section 18. Crimes Evidence Against One's Self Jeopardy

Section 19. Right to Bail Exceptions

Section 20. Excessive Bail, Fines or Punishment

Section 21. Suspension of Habeas Corpus

Section 22. Military Subject to Civil Power Quartering of Troops

Section 23. Trial by Jury Grand Jury

Section 24. Right to Assemble and Petition

Section 25. Due Process of Law

Section 26. Slavery Prohibited

Section 27. Property Rights of Aliens

Section 28. Rights Reserved Not Disparaged

Section 29. Equality of the Sexes

Section 30. Right to Vote or Petition on Annexation Enclaves

Section 30a. Official Language.

Section 30b. No Protected Status Based on Homosexual, Lesbian or Bisexual Orientation

Article III: Distribution of Powers – Page 52

Section 1. Distribution of Powers

Article IV: Executive Department – Page 53

Section 1. Officers Term of Office

Section 2. Governor Supreme Executive

Section 3. State Officers Election Returns.

Section 4. Qualifications of State Officers

Section 5. Governor Commander in Chief of Militia

Section 6. Appointment of Officers Vacancy

Section 7. Governor May Grant Reprieves and Pardons

Section 8. Governor May Require Information from Officers Message

Section 9. Governor May Convene Legislature or Senate

Section 10. Governor May Adjourn Legislature

Section 11. Bills Presented to Governor Veto Return

Section 12. Governor May Veto Items in Appropriation Bills Reconsideration

Section 13. Succession to the Office of Governor and Lieutenant Governor

Section 14. Lieutenant Governor President of Senate (Repealed)

Section 15. No Lieutenant Governor Who to Act as Governor.

Section 16. Account and Report of Moneys

Section 17. Executive Officers to Make Report (Repealed)

Section 18. State Seal

Section 19. Salaries of Officers Fees Paid into Treasury

Section 20. State Librarian (Repealed)

Section 21. Elected Auditor of State Powers and Duties (Repealed).

Section 22. Principal Departments (Repealed)

Section 23. Commissioner of Insurance

Article V: Legislative Department – Page 63

Section 1. General Assembly Initiative and Referendum

Section 2. Election of Members Oath Vacancies

Section 3. Terms of Senators and Representatives

Section 4. Qualifications of Members

Section 5. Classification of Senators

Section 6. Salary and Expenses of Members

Section 7. General Assembly Shall Meet When Term of Members Committees

Section 8. Members Precluded from Holding Office

Section 9. Increase of Salary When Forbidden (Repealed)

Section 10. Each House to Choose Its Officers

Section 11. Quorum

Section 12. Each House Makes and Enforces Rules

Section 13. Journal Ayes and Noes to be Entered, When

Section 14. Open Sessions

Section 15. Adjournment for More Than Three Days

Section 16. Privileges of Members

Section 17. No Law Passed but by Bill Amendments

Section 18. Enacting Clause

Section 19. When Laws Take Effect Introduction of Bills

Section 20. Bills Referred to Committee Printed

Section 21. Bill to Contain but One Subject Expressed in Title

Section 22. Reading and Passage of Bills

Section 22a. Caucus Positions Prohibited Penalties

Section 22b. Effect of Sections 20 and 22a

Section 23. Vote on Amendments and Report of Committee

Section 24. Revival, Amendment or Extension of Laws

Section 25. Special Legislation Prohibited

Section 25a. Eight-hour Employment

Section 26. Signing of Bills

Section 27. Officers and Employees Compensation

Section 28. Extra Compensation to Officers, Employees, or Contractors Forbidden

Section 29. Contracts for Facilities and Supplies

Section 30. Salary of Governor and Judges to be Fixed by Legislature Term Not to be Extended or Salaries Increased or Decreased (Repealed)

Section 31. Revenue Bills

Section 32. Appropriation Bills

Section 33. Disbursement of Public Money

Section 34. Appropriations to Private Institutions Forbidden

Section 35. Delegation of Power

Section 36. Laws on Investment of Trust Funds

Section 37. Change of Venue (Repealed)

Section 38. No Liability Exchanged or Released

Section 39. Orders and Resolutions Presented to Governor

Section 40. Bribery and Influence in General Assembly

Section 41. Offering, Giving, Promising Money or Other Consideration (Repealed)

Section 42. Corrupt Solicitation of Members and Officers (Repealed)

Section 43. Member Interested Shall Not Vote

Section 44. Representatives in Congress

Section 45. General Assembly

Section 46. Senatorial and Representative Districts

Section 47. Composition of Districts

Section 48. Revision and Alteration of Districts Reapportionment Commission

Section 49. Appointment of State Auditor Term Qualifications Duties

Section 50. Public Funding of Abortion Forbidden

Article VI: Judicial Department – Page 85

Section 1. Vestment of Judicial Power

Supreme Court

Section 2. Appellate Jurisdiction

Section 3. Original Jurisdiction Opinions

Section 4. Terms

Section 5. Personnel of Court Departments Chief Justice

Section 6. Election of Judges (Repealed)

Section 7. Term of Office

Section 8. Qualifications of Justices

District Courts

Section 9. District Courts Jurisdiction

Section 10. Judicial Districts District Judges

Section 11. Qualifications of District Judges

Section 12. Terms of Court

District Attorneys

Section 13. District Attorneys Election Term Salary Qualifications

Probates and Juvenile Courts

Section 14. Probate Court Jurisdiction Judges Election Term

Section 15. Juvenile Court Jurisdiction Judges Election Term

County Courts

Section 16. County Judges Terms Qualifications.

Section 17. County Courts Jurisdiction Appeals.

Miscellaneous

Section 18. Compensation and Services

Section 19. Laws Relating to Courts Uniform

Section 20. Vacancies

Section 21. Rule-making Power

Section 22. Process Prosecution In Name of People

Section 23. Retirement and Removal of Justices and Judges

Section 24. Judicial Nominating Commissions

Section 25. Election of Justices and Judges

Section 26. Denver County Judges

Article VII: Suffrage and Elections – Page 100

Section 1. Qualifications of Elector

Section 1a. Qualifications of Elector Residence on Federal Land

Section 2. Suffrage to Women (Repealed)

Section 3. Educational Qualifications of Elector (Deleted by amendment)

Section 4. When Residence Does Not Change

Section 5. Privilege of Voters

Section 6. Electors Only Eligible to Office

Section 7. General Election

Section 8. Elections by Ballot or Voting Machine

Section 9. No Privilege to Witness in Election Trial

Section 10. Disfranchisement During Imprisonment

Section 11. Purity of Elections

Section 12. Election Contests By Whom Tried

Article VIII: State Institutions – Page 103

Section 1. Established and Supported by State

Section 2. Seat of Government Where Located

Section 3. Seat of Government How Changed

Section 4. Appropriation for Capitol Building (Repealed)

Section 5. Educational Institutions

Article IX: Education – Page 106

Section 1. Supervision of Schools Board of Education

Section 2. Establishment and Maintenance of Public Schools

Section 3. School Fund Inviolate

Section 4. County Treasurer to Collect and Disburse

Section 5. Of What School Fund Consists

Section 6. County Superintendent of Schools

Section 7. Aid to Private Schools, Churches, Sectarian Purpose, Forbidden

Section 8. Religious Test and Race Discrimination Forbidden Sectarian Tenets

Section 9. State Board of Land Commissioners

Section 10. Selection and Control of Public Lands

Section 11. Compulsory Education

Section 12. Regents of University

Section 13. President of University

Section 14. Control of University (Repealed)

Section 15. School Districts Board of Education

Section 16. Textbooks in Public Schools

Article X: Revenue – Page 117

Section 1. Fiscal Year

Section 2. Tax Provided for State Expenses

Section 3. Uniform Taxation Exemptions

Section 4. Public Property Exempt

Section 5. Property Used for Religious Worship, Schools and Charitable Purposes Exempt

Section 6. Self-propelled Equipment, Motor Vehicles, and Certain Other Movable Equipment

Section 7. Municipal Taxation by General Assembly Prohibited

Section 8. No County, City, Town to be Released

Section 9. Relinquishment of Power to Tax Corporations Forbidden

Section 10. Corporations Subject to Tax

Section 11. Maximum Rate of Taxation

Section 12. Public Funds Report of State Treasurer

Section 13. Making Profit on Public Money Felony

Section 14. Private Property Not Taken for Public Debt

Section 15. Boards of Equalization Duties Property Tax Administrator

Section 16. Appropriations Not to Exceed Tax Exceptions

Section 17. Income Tax

Section 18. License Fees and Excise Taxes Use of

Section 19. State Income Tax Laws by Reference to United States Tax Laws

Section 20. The Taxpayer's Bill of Rights

Article XI: Public Indebtedness – Page 135

Section 1. Pledging Credit of State, County, City, Town or School District Forbidden

Section 2. No Aid to Corporations No Joint Ownership by State, County, City, Town, or School District

Section 2a. Student Loan Program

Section 3. Public Debt of State Limitations

Section 4. Law Creating Debt

Section 5. Debt for Public Buildings How Created

Section 6. Local Government Debt

Section 7. State and Political Subdivisions May Give Assistance to Any Political Subdivision

Section 8. City Indebtedness; Ordinance, Tax, Water Obligations Excepted

Section 9. This Article Not to Affect Prior Obligations (Repealed)

Section 10. 1976 Winter Olympics (Deleted by Amendment)

Article XII: Officers – Page 139

Section 1. When Office Expires Suspension by Law

Section 2. Personal Attention Required

Section 3. Defaulting Collector Disqualified from Office

Section 4. Disqualifications from Holding Office of Trust or Profit

Section 5. Investigation of State and County Treasurers

Section 6. Bribery of Officers Defined

Section 7. Bribery Corrupt Solicitation

Section 8. Oath of Civil Officers

Section 9. Oaths Where Filed

Section 10. Refusal to Qualify Vacancy

Section 11. Elected Public Officers Term Salary Vacancy

Section 12. Duel Disqualifies for Office (Deleted by Amendment)

Section 13. Personnel System of State Merit System

Section 14. State Personnel Board State Personnel Director

Section 15. Veterans' Preference

Article XIII: Impeachments – Page 150

Section 1. House Impeach Senate Try Conviction When Chief Justice Presides

Section 2. Who Liable to Impeachment Judgment No Bar to Prosecution

Section 3. Officers Not Subject to Impeachment Subject to Removal

Article XIV: Counties – Page 151

Section 1. Counties of State

Section 2. Removal of County Seats

Section 3. Striking Off Territory Vote

Section 4. New County Shall Pay Proportion of Debt

Section 5. Part Stricken Off Pay Proportion of Debt. County Officers

Section 6. County Commissioners Election Term

Section 7. Officers Compensation (Repealed)

Section 8. County Officers Election Term Salary

Section 9. Vacancies How Filled

Section 10. Elector Only Eligible to County Office

Section 11. Justices of the Peace Constables (Repealed)

Section 12. Other Officers

Section 13. Classification of Cities and Towns

Section 14. Existing Cities and Towns May Come Under General Law

Section 15. Compensation and Fees of County Officers

Section 16. County Home Rule

Section 17. Service Authorities

Section 18. Intergovernmental Relationships

Article XV: Corporations – Page 161

Section 1. Unused Charters or Grants of Privilege

Section 2. Corporate Charters Created by General Law

Section 3. Power to Revoke, Alter or Annul Charter

Section 4. Railroads Common Carriers Construction Intersection

Section 5. Consolidation of Parallel Lines Forbidden

Section 6. Equal Rights of Public to Transportation

Section 7. Existing Railroads to File Acceptance of Constitution

Section 8. Eminent Domain Police Power Not to be Abridged

Section 9. Fictitious Stock, Bonds Increase of Stock

Section 10. Foreign Corporations Place Agent

Section 11. Street Railroads Consent of Municipality

Section 12. Retrospective Laws Not to be Passed

Section 13. Telegraph Lines Consolidation

Section 14. Railroad or Telegraph Companies Consolidating with Foreign Companies

Section 15. Contracts with Employees Releasing from Liability Void

Article XVI: Mining and Irrigation – Page 165

Mines

Section 1. Commissioner of Mines

Section 2. Ventilation Employment of Children

Section 3. Drainage

Section 4. Mining, Metallurgy, in Public Institutions

Irrigation

Section 5. Water of Streams Public Property

Section 6. Diverting Unappropriated Water Priority Preferred Uses

Section 7. Right-of-way for Ditches, Flumes

Section 8. County Commissioners to Fix Rates for Water, When

Article XVII: Militia – Page 167

Section 1. Persons Subject to Service

Section 2. Organization Equipment Discipline

Section 3. Officers How Chosen

Section 4. Armories

Section 5. Exemption in Time of Peace

Article XVIII: Miscellaneous – Page 168

Section 1. Homestead and Exemption Laws

Section 2. Lotteries Prohibited Exceptions

Section 3. Arbitration Laws

Section 4. Felony Defined

Section 5. Spurious and Drugged Liquors Laws Concerning

Section 6. Preservation of Forests

Section 7. Land Value Increase Arboreal Planting Exempt

Section 8. Publication of Laws

Section 9. Limited Gaming Permitted

Section 9a. U.S. Senators and Representatives Limitation on Terms

Section 10. Severability of Constitutional Provisions

Section 11. Elected Government Officials -- Limitations on Terms

Section 12. Congressional Term Limits Amendment

Section 12a. Congressional Term Limits Declaration

Section 13. Prohibited Methods of Taking Wildlife

Article XIX: Amendments – Page 205

Section 1. Constitutional Convention How Called

Section 2. Amendments to Constitution How Adopted

Article XX: Home Rule Cities and Towns – Page 207

Section 1. Incorporated

Section 2. Officers

Section 3. Transfer of Government

Section 4. First Charter

Section 5. New Charters, Amendments or Measures

Section 6. Home Rule for Cities and Towns

Section 7. City and County of Denver Single School District Consolidations

Section 8. Conflicting Constitutional Provisions Declared Inapplicable

Section 9. Procedure and Requirements for Adoption

Section 10. City and county of Broomfield - created

Section 11. Officers - city and county of Broomfield

Section 12. Transfer of government

Section 13. Sections self-executing - appropriations

Article XXI: Recall from Office – Page 223

Section 1. State Officers May be Recalled

Section 2. Form of Recall Petition

Section 3. Resignation Filling Vacancy

Section 4. Limitation Municipal Corporations May Adopt, When

Article XXII: Intoxicating Liquors (repealed) – Page 229

Section 1. Repeal of Intoxicating Liquor Laws

Article XXIII: Publication of Legal Advertising (repealed) – Page 230

Section 1. Publication of Proposed Constitutional Amendments and Initiated and Referred Bills

Article XXIV: Old Age Pensions – Page 231

Section 1. Fund Created

Section 2. Moneys Allocated to Fund

Section 3. Persons Entitled to Receive Pensions

Section 4. The State Board of Public Welfare to Administer Fund

Section 5. Revenues for Old Age Pension Fund Continued

Section 6. Basic Minimum Award

Section 7. Stabilization Fund and Health and Medical Care Fund

Section 8. Fund to Remain Inviolate

Section 9. Effective Date

Article XXV: Public Utilities – Page 235

Section 1. Public Utilities

Article XXVI: Nuclear Detonations – Page 236

Section 1. Nuclear Detonations Prohibited Exceptions

Section 2. Election Required

Section 3. Certification of Indemnification Required

Section 4. Article Self-executing

Section 5. Severability

Article XXVII: Great Outdoors Colorado – Page 238

Section 1. Great Outdoors Colorado Program

Section 2. Trust Fund Created

Section 3. Moneys Allocated to Trust Fund

Section 4. Fund to Remain Inviolate

Section 5. Trust Fund Expenditures

Section 6. The State Board of the Great Outdoors Colorado Trust Fund

Section 7. No effect on Colorado water law

Section 8. No Substitution Allowed

Section 9. Eminent Domain

Section 10. Payment in lieu of Taxes

Section 11. Effective Date

Article XXVIII: Campaign and Political Finance – Page 246

Section 1. Purposes and Findings

Section 2. Definitions

Section 3. Contribution Limits

Section 4. Voluntary Campaign Spending Limits

Section 5. Independent Expenditures

Section 6. Electioneering Communications:

Section 7. Disclosures

Section 8. Filing - Where to File – Timeliness

Section 9. Duties of the Secretary of State – Enforcement

Section 10. Filing - Where to File – Timeliness

Section 11. Conflicting Provisions Declared Inapplicable

Section 12. Repeal of Conflicting Statutory Provisions

Section 13. Applicability and Effective Date

Section 14. Severability

Section 15. Presumption of Impropriety

Section 16. Enforcement

Section 17. Government Contracts

Article XXIX: Ethics in Government – Page 266

Section 1. Purposes and Findings

Section 2. Definitions

Section 3. Gift ban

Section 4. Restrictions on representation after leaving office

Section 5. Independent ethics commission

Section 6. Penalty

Section 7. Counties and Municipalities

Section 8. Conflicting provisions declared inapplicable

Section 9. Legislation to facilitate article

Schedule – Page 274

Section 1. All Laws Remain Till Repealed

Section 2. Contracts Recognizances Indictments

Section 3. Territorial Property Vests in State

Section 4. Duty of General Assembly

Section 5. Supreme and District Courts Transition

Section 6. Judges District Attorneys Term Commence on Filing Oath

Section 7. Seals of Supreme and District Courts

Section 8. Probate Court County Court

Section 9. Terms Probate Court, Probate Judge, Apply to County Court, County Judge

Section 10. County and Precinct Officers

Section 11. Vacancies in County Offices

Section 12. Constitution Takes Effect on President's Proclamation

Section 13. First Election, Contest

Section 14. First Election Canvass

Section 15. Senators Representatives Districts

Section 16. Congressional Election Canvass

Section 17. General Assembly, First Session Restrictions Removed

Section 18. First General Assembly Canvass

Section 19. Presidential Electors, 1876

Section 20. Presidential Electors After 1876

Section 21. Expenses of Convention

Section 22. Recognizances, Bonds, Payable to People Continue

Preamble:

We, the people of Colorado, with profound reverence for the Supreme Ruler of the Universe, in order to form a more independent and perfect government; establish justice; insure tranquility; provide for the common defense; promote the general welfare and secure the blessings of liberty to ourselves and our posterity, do ordain and establish this constitution for the "State of Colorado".

Article I: Boundaries

The boundaries of the state of Colorado shall be as follows: Commencing on the thirty-seventh parallel of north latitude, where the twenty-fifth meridian of longitude west from Washington crosses the same; thence north, on said meridian, to the forty-first parallel of north latitude; thence along said parallel, west, to the thirty-second meridian of longitude west from Washington; thence south, on said meridian, to the thirty-seventh parallel of north latitude; thence along said thirty-seventh parallel of north latitude to the place of beginning.

Article II: Bill of Rights

In order to assert our rights, acknowledge our duties, and proclaim the principles upon which our government is founded, we declare:

Section 1. Vestment of Political Power

All political power is vested in and derived from the people; all government, of right, originates from the people, is founded upon their will only, and is instituted solely for the good of the whole.

Section 2. People May Alter or Abolish Form of Government Proviso

The people of this state have the sole and exclusive right of governing themselves, as a free, sovereign and independent state; and to alter and abolish their constitution and form of government whenever they may deem it necessary to their safety and happiness, provided, such change be not repugnant to the constitution of the United States.

Section 3. Inalienable Rights

All persons have certain natural, essential and inalienable rights, among which may be reckoned the right of enjoying and defending their lives and liberties; of acquiring, possessing and protecting property; and of seeking and obtaining their safety and happiness.

Section 4. Religious Freedom

The free exercise and enjoyment of religious profession and worship, without discrimination, shall forever hereafter be guaranteed; and no person shall be denied any civil or political right, privilege or capacity, on account of his opinions concerning religion; but the liberty of conscience hereby secured shall not be construed to dispense with oaths or affirmations, excuse acts of licentiousness or justify practices inconsistent with the good order, peace or safety of the state. No person shall be required to attend or support any ministry or place of worship, religious sect or denomination against his consent. Nor shall any preference be given by law to any religious denomination or mode of worship.

Section 5. Freedom of Elections

All elections shall be free and open; and no power, civil or military, shall at any time interfere to prevent the free exercise of the right of suffrage.

Section 6. Equality of Justice

Courts of justice shall be open to every person, and a speedy remedy afforded for every injury to person, property or character; and right and justice should be administered without sale, denial or delay.

Section 7. Security of Person and Property -Searches -Seizures -Warrants

The people shall be secure in their persons, papers, homes and effects, from unreasonable searches and seizures; and no warrant to search any place or seize any person or things shall issue without describing the place to be searched, or the person or thing to be seized, as near as may be, nor without probable cause, supported by oath or affirmation reduced to writing.

Section 8. Prosecutions -Indictment or Information

Until otherwise provided by law, no person shall, for a felony, be proceeded against criminally otherwise than by indictment, except in cases arising in the land or naval forces, or in the militia when in actual service in time of war or public danger. In all other cases, offenses shall be prosecuted criminally by indictment or information.

Section 9. Treason-Estates of Suicides

Treason against the state can consist only in levying war against it or in adhering to its enemies, giving them aid and comfort; no person can be convicted of treason, unless on the testimony of two witnesses to the same overt act, or on his confession in open court; no person can be attainted of treason or felony by the general assembly; no conviction can work corruption of blood or forfeiture of estate; the estates of such persons as may destroy their own lives shall descend or vest as in cases of natural death.

Section 10. Freedom of Speech and Press

No law shall be passed impairing the freedom of speech; every person shall be free to speak, write or publish whatever he will on any subject, being responsible for all abuse of that liberty; and in all suits and prosecutions for libel the truth thereof may be given in evidence, and the jury, under the direction of the court, shall determine the law and the fact.

Section 11. Ex Post Facto Laws

No ex post facto law, nor law impairing the obligation of contracts, or retrospective in its operation, or making any irrevocable grant of special privileges, franchises or immunities, shall be passed by the general assembly.

Section 12. No Imprisonment for Debt

No person shall be imprisoned for debt, unless upon refusal to deliver up his estate for the benefit of his creditors in such manner as shall be prescribed by law, or in cases of tort or where there is a strong presumption of fraud.

Section 13. Right to Bear Arms

The right of no person to keep and bear arms in defense of his home, person and property, or in aid of the civil power when thereto legally summoned, shall be called in question; but nothing herein contained shall be construed to justify the practice of carrying concealed weapons.

Section 14. Taking Private Property for Private Use

Private property shall not be taken for private use unless by consent of the owner, except for private ways of necessity, and except for reservoirs, drains, flumes or ditches on or across the lands of others, for agricultural, mining, milling, domestic or sanitary purposes.

Section 15. Taking Property for Public Use -Compensation, How Ascertained

Private property shall not be taken or damaged, for public or private use, without just compensation. Such compensation shall be ascertained by a board of commissioners, of not less than three freeholders, or by a jury, when required by the owner of the property, in such manner as may be prescribed by law, and until the same shall be paid to the owner, or into court for the owner, the property shall not be needlessly disturbed, or the proprietary rights of the owner therein divested; and whenever an attempt is made to take private property for a use alleged to be public, the question whether the contemplated use be really public shall be a judicial question, and determined as such without regard to any legislative assertion that the use is public.

Section 16. Criminal Prosecutions -Rights of Defendant

In criminal prosecutions the accused shall have the right to appear and defend in person and by counsel; to demand the nature and cause of the accusation; to meet the witnesses against him face to face; to have process to compel the attendance of witnesses in his behalf, and a speedy public trial by an impartial jury of the county or district in which the offense is alleged to have been committed.

Section 16a. Rights of Crime Victims

Any person who is a victim of a criminal act, or such person's designee, legal guardian, or surviving immediate family members if such person is deceased, shall have the right to be heard when relevant, informed, and present at all critical stages of the criminal justice process. All terminology, including the term "critical stages," shall be defined by the general assembly.

Section 17. Imprisonment of Witnesses-Depositions-Form

No person shall be imprisoned for the purpose of securing his testimony in any case longer than may be necessary in order to take his deposition. If he can give security he shall be discharged; if he cannot give security his deposition shall be taken by some judge of the supreme, district or county court, at the earliest time he can attend, at some convenient place by him appointed for that purpose, of which time and place the accused and the attorney prosecuting for the people shall have reasonable notice. The accused shall have the right to appear in person and by counsel. If he has no counsel, the judge shall assign him one in his behalf only. On the completion of such examination the witness shall be discharged on his own recognizance, entered into before said judge, but such deposition shall not be used if in the opinion of the court the personal attendance of the witness might be procured by the prosecution, or is procured by the accused. No exception shall be taken to such deposition as to matters of form.

Section 18. Crimes -Evidence Against One's Self -Jeopardy

No person shall be compelled to testify against himself in a criminal case nor shall any person be twice put in jeopardy for the same offense. If the jury disagree, or if the judgment be arrested after the verdict, or if the judgment be reversed for error in law, the accused shall not be deemed to have been in jeopardy.

Section 19. Right to Bail-Exceptions

(1) All persons shall be bailable by sufficient sureties pending disposition of charges except:
(a) For capital offenses when proof is evident or presumption is great; or

(b) When, after a hearing held within ninety-six hours of arrest and upon reasonable notice, the court finds that proof is evident or presumption is great as to the crime alleged to have been committed and finds that the public would be placed in significant peril if the accused were released on bail and such person is accused in any of the following cases:

(I) A crime of violence, as may be defined by the general assembly, alleged to have been committed while on probation or parole resulting from the conviction of a crime of violence;
(II) A crime of violence, as may be defined by the general assembly, alleged to have been committed while on bail pending the disposition of a previous crime of violence charge for which probable cause has been found;

(III) A crime of violence, as may be defined by the general assembly, alleged to have been committed after two previous felony convictions, or one such previous felony conviction if such conviction was for a crime of violence, upon charges separately brought and tried under the laws of this state or under the laws of any other state, the United States, or any territory subject to the jurisdiction of the United States which, if committed in this state, would be a felony; or

(c) Deleted by amendment.

(2) Except in the case of a capital offense, if a person is denied bail under this section, the trial of the person shall be commenced not more than ninety days after the date on which bail is denied. If the trial is not commenced within ninety days and the delay is not attributable to the defense, the court shall immediately schedule a bail hearing and shall set the amount of the bail for the person.

(2.5) (a) The court may grant bail after a person is convicted, pending sentencing or appeal, only as provided by statute as enacted by the general assembly; except that no bail is allowed for persons convicted of:

(I) Murder;
(II) Any felony sexual assault involving the use of a deadly weapon;
(III) Any felony sexual assault committed against a child who is under fifteen years of age;
(IV) A crime of violence, as defined by statute enacted by the general assembly; or
(V) Any felony during the commission of which the person used a firearm.

(b) The court shall not set bail that is otherwise allowed pursuant to this subsection (2.5) unless the court finds that:

(I) The person is unlikely to flee and does not pose a danger to the safety of any person or the community; and
(II) The appeal is not frivolous or is not pursued for the purpose of delay.

(3) This section shall take effect January 1, 1995, and shall apply to offenses committed on or after said date.

Section 20. Excessive Bail, Fines or Punishment
Excessive bail shall not be required, nor excessive fines imposed, nor cruel and unusual punishments inflicted.

Section 21. Suspension of Habeas Corpus
The privilege of the writ of habeas corpus shall never be suspended, unless when in case of rebellion or invasion, the public safety may require it.

Section 22. Military Subject to Civil Power Quartering of Troops
The military shall always be in strict subordination to the civil power; no soldier shall, in time of peace, be quartered in any house without the consent of the owner, nor in time of war except in the manner prescribed by law.

Section 23. Trial by Jury -Grand Jury
The right of trial by jury shall remain inviolate in criminal cases; but a jury in civil cases in all courts, or in criminal cases in courts not of record, may consist of less than twelve persons, as may be prescribed by law. Hereafter a grand jury shall consist of twelve persons, any nine of whom concurring may find an indictment; provided, the general assembly may change, regulate or abolish the grand jury system; and provided, further, the right of any person to serve on any jury shall not be denied or abridged on account of sex, and the general assembly may

provide by law for the exemption from jury service of persons or classes of persons.

Section 24. Right to Assemble and Petition
The people have the right peaceably to assemble for the common good, and to apply to those invested with the powers of government for redress of grievances, by petition or remonstrance.

Section 25. Due Process of Law
No person shall be deprived of life, liberty or property, without due process of law.

Section 26. Slavery Prohibited
There shall never be in this state either slavery or involuntary servitude, except as a punishment for crime, whereof the party shall have been duly convicted.

Section 27. Property Rights of Aliens
Aliens, who are or may hereafter become bona fide residents of this state, may acquire, inherit, possess, enjoy and dispose of property, real and personal, as native born citizens.

Section 28. Rights Reserved Not Disparaged
The enumeration in this constitution of certain rights shall not be construed to deny, impair or disparage others retained by the people.

Section 29. Equality of the Sexes
Equality of rights under the law shall not be denied or abridged by the state of Colorado or any of its political subdivisions on account of sex.

Section 30. Right to Vote or Petition on Annexation -Enclaves

(1) No unincorporated area may be annexed to a municipality unless one of the following conditions first has been met:

(a) The question of annexation has been submitted to the vote of the landowners and the registered electors in the area proposed to be annexed, and the majority of such persons voting on the question have voted for the annexation; or
(b) The annexing municipality has received a petition for the annexation of such area signed by persons comprising more than fifty percent of the landowners in the area and owning more than fifty percent of the area, excluding public streets, and alleys and any land owned by the annexing municipality; or
(c) The area is entirely surrounded by or is solely owned by the annexing municipality.

(2) The provisions of this section shall not apply to annexations to the city and county of Denver, to the extent that such annexations are governed by other provisions of the constitution.
(3) The general assembly may provide by law for procedures necessary to implement this section. This section shall take effect upon completion of the canvass of votes taken thereon.

Section 30a. Official language
The English language is the official language of the State of Colorado.

This section is self executing; however, the General Assembly may enact laws to implement this section.

Section 30b. No Protected Status Based on Homosexual, Lesbian or Bisexual Orientation *[Declared to violate the United States Constitution by the United States Supreme Court in 1996. Not in force.]*
Neither the State of Colorado, through any of its branches or departments, nor any of its agencies, political subdivisions, municipalities or school districts, shall enact, adopt or enforce any statute, regulation, ordinance or policy whereby homosexual, lesbian or bisexual orientation, conduct, practices or relationships shall constitute or otherwise be the basis of or entitle any person or class of persons to have or claim any minority status, quota preferences, protected status or claim of discrimination. This Section of the Constitution shall be in all respects self-executing.

Section 31. Marriages: Valid or recognized:
Only a union of one man and one woman shall be valid or recognized as a marriage in this state.

Article III: Distribution of Powers

The powers of the government of this state are divided into three distinct departments,--the legislative, executive and judicial; and no person or collection of persons charged with the exercise of powers properly belonging to one of these departments shall exercise any power properly belonging to either of the others, except as in this constitution expressly directed or permitted.

Article IV: Executive Department

Section 1. Officers Term of Office

(1) The executive department shall include the governor, lieutenant governor, secretary of state, state treasurer, and attorney general, each of whom shall hold his office for the term of four years, commencing on the second Tuesday of January in the year 1967, and each fourth year thereafter. They shall perform such duties as are prescribed by this constitution or by law.

(2) In order to broaden the opportunities for public service and to guard against excessive concentrations of power, no governor, lieutenant governor, secretary of state, state treasurer, or attorney general shall serve more than two consecutive terms in such office. This limitation on the number of terms shall apply to terms of office beginning on or after January 1, 1991. Any person who succeeds to the office of governor or is appointed or elected to fill a vacancy in one of the other offices named in this section, and who serves at least one- half of a term of office, shall be considered to have served a term in that office for purposes of this subsection (2). Terms are considered consecutive unless they are at least four years apart.

Section 2. Governor Supreme Executive
The supreme executive power of the state shall be vested in the governor, who shall take care that the laws be faithfully executed.

Section 3. State Officers Election Returns.
The officers named in section one of this article shall be chosen on the day of the general election, by the registered electors of the state. The governor and the lieutenant governor shall be chosen jointly by the casting by each voter of a single vote applicable to both offices. The returns of every election for said

officers shall be sealed up and transmitted to the secretary of state, directed to the speaker of the house of representatives, who shall immediately, upon the organization of the house, and before proceeding to other business, open and publish the same in the presence of a majority of the members of both houses of the general assembly, who shall for that purpose assemble in the house of representatives. The joint candidates having the highest number of votes cast for governor and lieutenant governor, and the person having the highest number of votes for any other office, shall be declared duly elected, but if two or more have an equal and the highest number of votes for the same office or offices, one of them, or any two for whom joint votes were cast for governor and lieutenant governor respectively, shall be chosen thereto by the two houses, on joint ballot. Contested elections for the said offices shall be determined by the two houses, on joint ballot, in such manner as may be prescribed by law.

Section 4. Qualifications of State Officers
No person shall be eligible to the office of governor or lieutenant governor unless he shall have attained the age of thirty years, nor to the office of secretary of state or state treasurer unless he shall have attained the age of twenty- five years, nor to the office of attorney general unless he shall have attained the age of twenty -five years and be a licensed attorney of the supreme court of the state in good standing, and no person shall be eligible to any one of said offices unless, in addition to the qualifications above prescribed therefore, he shall be a citizen of the United States, and have resided within the limits of the state two years next preceding his election.

Section 5. Governor Commander in Chief of Militia
The governor shall be commander-n-chief of the military forces of the state, except when they shall be called into actual service of the United States. He shall have power to call out the militia to execute the laws, suppress insurrection or repel invasion.

Section 6. Appointment of Officers Vacancy

(1) The governor shall nominate, and, by and with the consent of the senate, appoint all officers whose offices are established by this constitution, or which may be created by law, and whose appointment or election is not otherwise provided for, and may remove any such officer for incompetency, neglect of duty, or malfeasance in office. If the vacancy occurs in any such office while the senate is not in session, the governor shall appoint some fit person to discharge the duties thereof until the next meeting of the senate when he shall nominate and, by and with the consent of the senate, appoint some fit person to fill such office.

(2) If the office of state treasurer, secretary of state, or attorney general shall be vacated by death, resignation, or otherwise, the governor shall nominate and, by and with the consent of the senate, appoint a successor. The appointee shall hold the office until his successor shall be elected and qualified in such manner as may be provided by law. If the vacancy occurs in any such office while the senate is not in session, the governor shall appoint some fit person to discharge the duties thereof until the next meeting of the senate, when he shall nominate and, by and with the consent of the senate, appoint some fit person to fill such office.

(3) The senate in deliberating upon executive nominations may sit with closed doors, but in acting upon nominations they shall sit with open doors, and the vote shall be taken by ayes and noes, which shall be entered upon the journal.

Section 7. Governor May Grant Reprieves and Pardons

The governor shall have power to grant reprieves, commutations and pardons after conviction, for all offenses except treason, and except in case of impeachment, subject to such regulations as may be prescribed by law relative to the manner of applying for pardons, but he shall in every case where he may exercise this power, send to the general assembly at its first session thereafter, a transcript of the petition, all proceedings, and the reasons for his action.

Section 8. Governor May Require Information from Officers Message

The governor may require information in writing from the officers of the executive department upon any subject relating to the duties of their respective offices, which information shall be given upon oath whenever so required; he may also require information in writing at any time, under oath, from all officers and managers of state institutions, upon any subject relating to the condition, management and expenses of their respective offices and institutions. The governor shall, at the commencement of each session, and from time to time, by message, give to the general assembly information of the condition of the state, and shall recommend such measures as he shall deem expedient. He shall also send to the general assembly a statement, with vouchers, of the expenditures of all moneys belonging to the state and paid out by him. He shall, also, at the commencement of each session, present estimates of the amount of money required to be raised by taxation for all purposes of the state.

Section 9. Governor May Convene Legislature or Senate

The governor may, on extraordinary occasions convene the general assembly, by proclamation, stating therein the purpose for which it is to assemble; but at such special session no business shall be transacted other than that specially named in the proclamation. He may by proclamation, convene the senate in extraordinary session for the transaction of executive business.

Section 10. Governor May Adjourn Legislature

The governor, in case of a disagreement between the two houses as to the time of adjournment, may upon the same being certified to him by the house last moving adjournment, adjourn the general assembly to a day not later than the first day of the next regular session.

Section 11. Bills Presented to Governor Veto Return

Every bill passed by the general assembly shall, before it becomes a law, be presented to the governor. If he approve, he shall sign it, and thereupon it shall become a law; but if he do not approve, he shall return it, with his objections, to the house in which it originated, which house shall enter the objections at large upon its journal, and proceed to reconsider the bill. If then two- thirds of the members elected agree to pass the same, it shall be sent, together with the objections, to the other house, by which it shall likewise be reconsidered, and if approved by two- thirds of the members elected to that house, it shall become a law, notwithstanding the objections of the governor. In all such cases the vote of each house shall be determined by ayes and noes, to be entered upon the journal. If any bill shall not be returned by the governor within ten days after it shall have been presented to him, the same shall be a law in like manner as if he had signed it, unless the general assembly shall by their adjournment prevent its return, in which case it shall be filed with his objections in the office of the secretary of state, within thirty days after such adjournment, or else become a law.

Section 12. Governor May Veto Items in Appropriation Bills Reconsideration

The governor shall have power to disapprove of any item or items of any bill making appropriations of money, embracing distinct items, and the part or parts of the bill approved shall be law, and the item or items disapproved shall be void, unless enacted in manner following: If the general assembly be in session, he shall transmit to the house in which the bill originated a copy of the item or items thereof disapproved, together with his objections thereto, and the items objected to shall be separately reconsidered, and each item shall then take the same course as is prescribed for the passage of bills over the executive veto.

Section 13. Succession to the Office of Governor and Lieutenant Governor

(1) In the case of the death, impeachment, conviction of a felony, or resignation of the governor, the office of governor shall be vacant and the lieutenant governor shall take the oath of office and shall become governor.

(2) Whenever there is a vacancy in the office of the lieutenant governor, because of death, impeachment, conviction of a felony, or resignation, the governor shall nominate a lieutenant governor who shall take office upon confirmation by a majority vote of both houses of the general assembly. If the person nominated is a member of the general assembly, he may take the oath of office of lieutenant governor, and the legislative seat to which he was elected shall be vacant and filled in the manner prescribed by law pursuant to section 2 of article V of this constitution.

(3) In the event that the governor -elect fails to assume the office of governor because of death, resignation, or conviction of a felony, or refuses to take the oath of office, the lieutenant governor -elect shall take the oath of office and shall become governor on the second Tuesday in January in accordance with the provisions of section 1 of article IV of this constitution. In the event the lieutenant governor -elect fails to assume the office of lieutenant governor because of death, resignation, or conviction of a felony, or refuses to take the oath of office, the governor-elect upon taking office shall nominate a lieutenant governor who shall take the oath of office upon confirmation by a majority vote of both houses of the general assembly. If the person nominated is a member of the general assembly, he may take the oath of office of lieutenant governor, and the legislative seat to which he was elected shall be vacant and filled in the manner prescribed by law pursuant to section 2 of article V of this constitution.

(4) In the event the lieutenant governor or lieutenant governor-elect accedes to the office of governor because of a vacancy in said office for any of the causes enumerated in subsections (1) and (3) of this section, the office of lieutenant governor shall be vacant. Upon taking office, the new governor shall nominate a lieutenant governor who shall take the oath of office upon confirmation by a majority vote of both houses of the general assembly. If the person nominated is a member of the general assembly, he may take the oath of office of lieutenant governor, and the legislative seat to which he was elected shall be vacant and filled in the manner prescribed by law pursuant to section 2 of article V of this constitution.

(5) In the event the governor or lieutenant governor, or governor -elect or lieutenant governor -elect, at the time either of the latter is to take the oath of office, is absent from the state or is suffering from a physical or mental disability, the powers and duties of the office of governor and the office of lieutenant governor shall, until the absence or disability ceases, temporarily devolve upon the lieutenant governor, in the case of the governor, and, in the case of the lieutenant governor, upon the first named member of the general assembly listed in subsection (7) of this section who is affiliated with the same political party as the lieutenant governor; except that if the lieutenant governor and none of said members of the general assembly are affiliated with the same political party, the temporary vacancy in the office of lieutenant governor shall be filled by the first named member in said subsection (7). In the event that the offices of both the governor and lieutenant governor are vacant at the same time for any of the reasons enumerated in this subsection (5), the successors to fill the vacancy in the office of governor and in the office of lieutenant governor shall be, respectively, the first and second named members of the general assembly listed in subsection (7) of this section who are affiliated with the same political party as the governor; except that if the governor and none of said members of the general assembly are affiliated with the same political party, the vacancy in the office of governor and the vacancy in the office of lieutenant governor, respectively, shall be filled by the first and second named members in said subsection (7). The pro rata salary of the governor or lieutenant governor shall be paid to his successor for as long as he serves in such capacity, during which time he shall receive no other salary from the state.

(6) The governor or governor- elect, lieutenant governor or lieutenant governor -elect, or person acting as governor or lieutenant governor may transmit to the president of the senate and the speaker of the house of representatives his written declaration that he suffers from a physical or mental disability and he is unable to properly discharge the powers and duties of the office of governor or lieutenant governor. In the event no such written declaration has been made, his physical or mental disability shall be determined by a majority of the supreme court after a hearing held pursuant to a joint request submitted by joint resolution adopted by two-thirds of all members of each house of the general assembly. Such determination shall be final and conclusive. The supreme court, upon its own initiative, shall determine if and when such disability ceases.

(7) In the event that the offices of both the governor and lieutenant governor are vacant at the same time for any of the reasons enumerated in subsections (1), (2), and (3) of this section, the successor to fill the vacancy in the office of governor shall be the first named of the following members of the general assembly who is affiliated with the same political party as the governor: President of the senate, speaker of the house of representatives, minority leader of the senate, or minority leader of the house of representatives; except that if the governor and none of said members of the general assembly are affiliated with the same political party, the vacancy shall be filled by one such member in the order of precedence listed in this subsection (7). The member filling the vacancy pursuant to this subsection (7) shall take the oath of office of governor and shall become governor. The office of lieutenant governor shall be filled in the same manner as prescribed in subsection (3) of this section when the lieutenant governor elect fails to assume the office of lieutenant governor.

Section 14. Lieutenant Governor President of Senate
Repealed November 5, 1974 by Colorado Amendment 6 (1974).

Section 15. No Lieutenant Governor Who to Act as Governor.

Repealed.

Section 16. Account and Report of Moneys
An account shall be kept by the officers of the executive department and of all public institutions of the state, of all moneys received by them severally from all sources, and for every service performed, and of all moneys disbursed by them severally, and a semi-annual report thereof shall be made to the governor, under oath.

Section 17. Executive Officers to Make Report

Repealed.

Section 18. State Seal
There shall be a seal of the state, which shall be kept by the secretary of state, shall be called the "Great Seal of the State of Colorado," and shall be in the form prescribed by the general assembly.

Section 19. Salaries of Officers Fees Paid into Treasury
The officers named in section one of this article shall receive for their services a salary to be established by law, which shall not be increased or diminished during their official terms. It shall be the duty of all such officers to collect in advance all fees prescribed by law for services rendered by them severally, and pay the same into the state treasury.

Section 20. State Librarian

Repealed.

Section 21. Elected Auditor of State Powers and Duties
Repealed November 5, 1974 -by Colorado Amendment 6 (1974)

Section 22. Principal Departments

Repealed.

Section 23. Commissioner of Insurance
The governor shall nominate and, by and with the consent of the senate, appoint the commissioner of insurance to serve at his pleasure, and the state personnel system shall not extend to the commissioner of insurance.

Article V: Legislative Department

General Assembly Initiative and Referendum.

(1) The legislative power of the state shall be vested in the general assembly consisting of a senate and house of representatives, both to be elected by the people, but the people reserve to themselves the power to propose laws and amendments to the constitution and to enact or reject the same at the polls independent of the general assembly and also reserve power at their own option to approve or reject at the polls any act or item, section, or part of any act of the general assembly.

(2) The first power hereby reserved by the people is the initiative, and signatures by registered electors in an amount equal to at least five percent of the total number of votes cast for all candidates for the office of secretary of state at the previous general election shall be required to propose any measure by petition, and every such petition shall include the full text of the measure so proposed. Initiative petitions for state legislation and amendments to the constitution, in such form as may be prescribed pursuant to law, shall be addressed to and filed with the secretary of state at least three months before the general election at which they are to be voted upon.

(2.5) In order to make it more difficult to amend this constitution, a petition for an initiated constitutional amendment shall be signed by registered electors who reside in each state senate district in Colorado in an amount equal to at least two percent of the total registered electors in the senate district provided that the total number of signatures of registered electors on the petition shall at least equal the number of signatures required by subsection (2) of this section. For purposes of this subsection (2.5), the number and boundaries of the senate districts and the number of registered electors in the senate districts shall be those in effect at the time the form of the petition has been approved for circulation as provided by law.

(3) The second power hereby reserved is the referendum, and it may be ordered, except as to laws necessary for the immediate preservation of the public peace, health, or safety, and appropriations for the support and maintenance of the departments of state and state institutions, against any act or item, section, or part of any act of the general assembly, either by a petition signed by registered electors in an amount equal to at least five percent of the total number of votes cast for all candidates for the office of the secretary of state at the previous general election or by the general assembly. Referendum petitions, in such form as may be prescribed pursuant to law, shall be addressed to and filed with the secretary of state not more than ninety days after the final adjournment of the session of the general assembly that passed the bill on which the referendum is demanded. The filing of a referendum petition against any item, section, or part of any act shall not delay the remainder of the act from becoming operative.

(4) (a) The veto power of the governor shall not extend to measures initiated by or referred to the people. All elections on measures initiated by or referred to the people of the state shall be held at the biennial regular general election, and all such measures shall become the law or a part of the constitution, when approved by a majority of the votes cast thereon or, if applicable the number of votes required pursuant to paragraph (b) of this subsection (4), and not otherwise, and shall take effect from and after the date of the official declaration of the vote thereon by proclamation of the governor, but not later than thirty days after the vote has been canvassed. This section shall not be construed to deprive the general assembly of the power to enact any measure.

(b) In order to make it more difficult to amend this constitution, an initiated constitutional amendment shall not become part of this constitution unless the amendment is approved by at least fifty-five percent of the votes cast thereon; except that this paragraph (b) shall not apply to an initiated constitutional amendment that is limited to repealing, in whole or in part, any provision of this constitution.

(5) The original draft of the text of proposed initiated constitutional amendments and initiated laws shall be submitted to the legislative research and drafting offices of the general assembly for review and comment. No later than two weeks after submission of the original draft, unless withdrawn by the proponents, the legislative research and drafting offices of the general assembly shall render their comments to the proponents of the proposed measure at a meeting open to the public, which shall be held only after full and timely notice to the public. Such meeting shall be held prior to the fixing of a ballot title. Neither the general assembly nor its committees or agencies shall have any power to require the amendment, modification, or other alteration of the text of any such proposed measure or to establish deadlines for the submission of the original draft of the text of any proposed measure.

(5.5) No measure shall be proposed by petition containing more than one subject, which shall be clearly expressed in its title; but if any subject shall be embraced in any measure which shall not be expressed in the title, such measure shall be void only as to so much thereof as shall not be so expressed. If a measure contains more than one subject, such that a ballot title cannot be fixed that clearly expresses a single subject, no title shall be set and the measure shall not be submitted to the people for adoption or rejection at the polls. In such circumstance, however, the measure may be revised and resubmitted for the fixing of a proper title without the necessity of review and comment on the revised measure in accordance with subsection (5) of this section, unless the revisions involve more than the elimination of provisions to achieve a single subject, or unless the official or officials responsible for the fixing of a title determine that the revisions are so substantial that such review and comment is in the public interest. The revision and resubmission of a measure in accordance with this subsection (5.5) shall not operate to alter or extend any filing deadline applicable to the measure.

(6) The petition shall consist of sheets having such general form printed or written at the top thereof as shall be designated or prescribed by the secretary of state; such petition shall be signed by registered electors in their own proper persons only, to which shall be attached the residence address of such person and the date of signing the same. To each of such petitions, which may consist of one or more sheets, shall be attached an affidavit of some registered elector that each signature thereon is the signature of the person whose name it purports to be and that, to the best of the knowledge and belief of the affiant, each of the persons signing said petition was, at the time of signing, a registered elector. Such petition so verified shall be prima facie evidence that the signatures thereon are genuine and true and that the persons signing the same are registered electors.

(7) The secretary of state shall submit all measures initiated by or referred to the people for adoption or rejection at the polls, in compliance with this section. In submitting the same and in all matters pertaining to the form of all petitions, the secretary of state and all other officers shall be guided by the general laws.

(7.3) Before any election at which the voters of the entire state will vote on any initiated or referred constitutional amendment or legislation, the nonpartisan research staff of the general assembly shall cause to be published the text and title of every such measure. Such publication shall be made at least one time in at least one legal publication of general circulation in each county of the state and shall be made at least fifteen days prior to the final date of voter registration for the election. The form and manner of publication shall be as prescribed by law and shall ensure a reasonable opportunity for the voters statewide to become informed about the text and title of each measure.

(7.5) (a) Before any election at which the voters of the entire state will vote on any initiated or referred constitutional amendment or legislation, the nonpartisan research staff of the general assembly shall prepare and make available to the public the following information in the form of a ballot information booklet:

(I) The text and title of each measure to be voted on;

(II) A fair and impartial analysis of each measure, which shall include a summary and the major arguments both for and against the measure, and which may include any other information that would assist understanding the purpose and effect of the measure. Any person may file written comments for consideration by the research staff during the preparation of such analysis.

(b) At least thirty days before the election, the research staff shall cause the ballot information booklet to be distributed to active registered voters statewide.

(c) If any measure to be voted on by the voters of the entire state includes matters arising under section 20 of article X of this constitution, the ballot information booklet shall include the information and the titled notice required by section 20 (3) (b) of article X, and the mailing of such information pursuant to section 20 (3) (b) of article X is not required.

(d) The general assembly shall provide sufficient appropriations for the preparation and distribution of the ballot information booklet pursuant to this subsection (7.5) at no charge to recipients.

(8) The style of all laws adopted by the people through the initiative shall be, "Be it Enacted by the People of the State of Colorado."

(9) The initiative and referendum powers reserved to the people by this section are hereby further reserved to the registered electors of every city, town, and municipality as to all local, special, and municipal legislation of every character in or for their respective municipalities. The manner of exercising said powers shall be prescribed by general laws; except that cities, towns, and municipalities may provide for the manner of exercising the initiative and referendum powers as to their municipal legislation. Not more than ten percent of the registered electors may be required to order the referendum, nor more than fifteen per cent to propose any measure by the initiative in any city, town, or municipality.

(10) This section of the constitution shall be in all respects self-executing; except that the form of the initiative or referendum petition may be prescribed pursuant to law.

Section 2. Election of Members Oath Vacancies.

(1) A general election for members of the general assembly shall be held on the first Tuesday after the first Monday in November in each even- numbered year, at such places in each county as now are or hereafter may be provided by law.

(2) Each member of the general assembly, before he enters upon his official duties, shall take an oath or affirmation to support the constitution of the United States and of the state of Colorado and to faithfully perform the duties of his office according to the best of his ability. This oath or affirmation shall be administered in the chamber of the house to which the member has been elected.

(3) Any vacancy occurring in either house by death, resignation, or otherwise shall be filled in the manner prescribed by law. The person appointed to fill the vacancy shall be a member of the same political party, if any, as the person whose termination of membership in the general assembly created the vacancy.

Section 3. Terms of Senators and Representatives.

(1) Senators shall be elected for the term of four years and representatives for the term of two years.

(2) In order to broaden the opportunities for public service and to assure that the general assembly is representative of Colorado citizens, no senator shall serve more than two consecutive terms in the senate, and no representative shall serve more than four consecutive terms in the house of representatives. This limitation on the number of terms shall apply to terms of office beginning on or after January 1, 1991. Any person appointed or elected to fill a vacancy in the general assembly and who serves at least one- half of a term of office shall be considered to have served a term in that office for purposes of this subsection (2). Terms are considered consecutive unless they are at least four years apart.

Section 4. Qualifications of Members.
No person shall be a representative or senator who shall not have attained the age of twenty-five years, who shall not be a citizen of the United States, and who shall not for at least twelve months next preceding his election, have resided within the territory included in the limits of the district in which he shall be chosen.

Section 5. Classification of Senators.
The senate shall be divided so that one -half of the senators, as nearly as practicable, may be chosen biennially.

Section 6. Salary and Expenses of Members.
Each member of the general assembly shall receive such salary and expenses as are prescribed by law. No general assembly shall fix its own salary. Members of the general assembly shall receive the same mileage rate permitted for travel as other state employees.

Section 7. General Assembly Shall Meet when Term of Members Committees.
General assembly - shall meet when - term of members - committees. The general assembly shall meet in regular session at 10 a.m. no later than the second Wednesday of January of each year. The general assembly shall meet at other times when convened in special session by the governor pursuant to section 9 of article IV of this constitution or by written request by two-thirds of the members of each house to the presiding officer of each house to consider only those subjects specified in such request. The term of service of the members of the general assembly shall begin on the convening of the first regular session of the general assembly next after their election. The committees of the general assembly, unless otherwise provided by the general assembly, shall expire on the convening of the first regular session after a general election. Regular sessions of the general assembly shall not exceed one hundred twenty calendar days.

Section 8. Members Precluded from Holding Office.
No senator or representative shall, while serving as such, be appointed to any civil office under this state; and no member of congress, or other person holding any office (except of attorney-at- law, notary public, or in the militia) under the United States or this state, shall be a member of either house during his continuance in office.

Section 9. Increase of Salary When Forbidden.

Repealed.

Section 10. Each House to Choose its Officers.
At the beginning of the first regular session after a general election, and at such other times as may be necessary, the senate shall elect one of its members president, and the house of representatives shall elect one of its members as speaker. The

president and speaker shall serve as such until the election and installation of their respective successors. Each house shall choose its other officers and shall judge the election and qualification of its members.

Section 11. Quorum.
A majority of each house shall constitute a quorum, but a smaller number may adjourn from day to day, and compel the attendance of absent members.

Section 12. Each House Makes and Enforces Rules.
Each house shall have power to determine the rules of its proceedings and adopt rules providing punishment of its members or other persons for contempt or disorderly behavior in its presence; to enforce obedience to its process; to protect its members against violence, or offers of bribes or private solicitation, and, with the concurrence of two-thirds, to expel a member, but not a second time for the same cause, and shall have all other powers necessary for the legislature of a free state. A member expelled for corruption shall not thereafter be eligible to either house of the same general assembly, and punishment for contempt or disorderly behavior shall not bar a prosecution for the same offense.

Section 13. Journal Ayes and Noes to Be Entered When.
Each house shall keep a journal of its proceedings and publish the same, except such parts as require secrecy, and the ayes and noes on any question shall, at the desire of any two members, be entered on the journal.

Section 14. Open Sessions.
The sessions of each house, and of the committees of the whole, shall be open, unless when the business is such as ought to be kept secret.

Section 15. Adjournment for More Than Three Days.
Neither house shall, without the consent of the other, adjourn for more than three days, nor to any other place than that in which the two houses shall be sitting.

Section 16. Privileges of Members.
The members of the general assembly shall, in all cases except treason or felony, be privileged from arrest during their attendance at the sessions of their respective houses, or any committees thereof, and in going to and returning from the same; and for any speech or debate in either house, or any committees thereof, they shall not be questioned in any other place.

Section 17. No Law Passed but by Bill Amendments.
No law shall be passed except by bill, and no bill shall be so altered or amended on its passage through either house as to change its original purpose.

Section 18. Enacting Clause.
The style of the laws of this state shall be: "Be it enacted by the General Assembly of the State of Colorado.

Section 19. When Laws Take Effect Introduction of Bills.
An act of the general assembly shall take effect on the date stated in the act, or, if no date is stated in the act, then on its passage. A bill may be introduced at any time during the session unless limited by action of the general assembly. No bill shall be introduced by title only.

Section 20. Bills Referred to Committee Printed.
No bill shall be considered or become a law unless referred to a committee, returned therefrom, and printed for the use of the members. Every measure referred to a committee of reference of

either house shall be considered by the committee upon its merits, and no rule of either house shall deny the opportunity for consideration and vote by a committee of reference upon such a measure within appropriate deadlines. A motion that the committee report the measure favorably to the committee of the whole, with or without amendments, shall always be in order within appropriate deadlines. Each measure reported to the committee of the whole shall appear on the appropriate house calendar in the order in which it was reported out of the committee of reference and within appropriate deadlines.

Section 21. Bill to Contain but One Subject Expressed in Title.
No bill, except general appropriation bills, shall be passed containing more than one subject, which shall be clearly expressed in its title; but if any subject shall be embraced in any act which shall not be expressed in the title, such act shall be void only as to so much thereof as shall not be so expressed.

Section 22. Reading and Passage of Bills.
Every bill shall be read by title when introduced, and at length on two different days in each house; provided, however, any reading at length may be dispensed with upon unanimous consent of the members present. All substantial amendments made thereto shall be printed for the use of the members before the final vote is taken on the bill, and no bill shall become a law except by a vote of the majority of all members elected to each house taken on two separate days in each house, nor unless upon its final passage the vote be taken by ayes and noes and the names of those voting be entered on the journal.

Section 22a. Caucus Positions Prohibited Penalties.
(1) No member or members of the general assembly shall require or commit themselves or any other member or members, through a vote in a party caucus or any other similar procedure,

to vote in favor of or against any bill, appointment, veto, or other measure or issue pending or proposed to be introduced in the general assembly.

(2) Notwithstanding the provisions of subsection (1) of this section, a member or members of the general assembly may vote in party caucus on matters directly relating to the selection of officers of a party caucus and the selection of the leadership of the general assembly.

Section 22b. Effect of Sections 20 and 22a.
Any action taken in violation of section 20 or 22a of this constitution shall be null and void.

Section 23. Vote on Amendments and Report of Committee.
No amendment to any bill by one house shall be concurred in by the other nor shall the report of any committee of conference be adopted in either house except by a vote of a majority of the members elected thereto, taken by ayes and noes, and the names of those voting recorded upon the journal thereof.

Section 24. Revival, Amendment or Extension of Laws.
No law shall be revived, or amended, or the provisions thereof extended or conferred by reference to its title only, but so much thereof as is revived, amended, extended or conferred, shall be re-enacted and published at length.

Section 25. Special Legislation Prohibited.
The general assembly shall not pass local or special laws in any of the following enumerated cases, that is to say; for granting divorces; laying out, opening, altering or working roads or highways; vacating roads, town plats, streets, alleys and public grounds; locating or changing county seats; regulating county or

township affairs; regulating the practice in courts of justice; regulating the jurisdiction and duties of justices of the peace, police magistrates and constables; changing the rules of evidence in any trial or inquiry; providing for changes of venue in civil or criminal cases; declaring any person of age; for limitation of civil actions or giving effect to informal or invalid deeds; summoning or impaneling grand or petit juries; providing for the management of common schools; regulating the rate of interest on money; the opening or conducting of any election, or designating the place of voting; the sale or mortgage of real estate belonging to minors or others under disability; the protection of game or fish; chartering or licensing ferries or toll bridges; remitting fines, penalties or forfeitures; creating, increasing or decreasing fees, percentage or allowances of public officers; changing the law of descent; granting to any corporation, association or individual the right to lay down railroad tracks; granting to any corporation, association or individual any special or exclusive privilege, immunity or franchise whatever. In all other cases, where a general law can be made applicable no special law shall be enacted.

Section 25a. Eight hour Employment.

(1) The general assembly shall provide by law, and shall prescribe suitable penalties for the violation thereof, for a period of employment not to exceed eight (8) hours within any twenty-four (24) hours (except in cases of emergency where life or property is in imminent danger) for persons employed in underground mines or other underground workings, blast furnaces, smelters; and any ore reduction works or other branch of industry or labor that the general assembly may consider injurious or dangerous to health, life or limb.

(2) The provisions of subsection (1) of this section to the contrary notwithstanding, the general assembly may establish whatever exceptions it deems appropriate to the eight-hour workday.

Section 26. Signing of Bills.
The presiding officer of each house shall sign all bills and joint resolutions passed by the general assembly, and the fact of signing shall be entered on or appended to the journal thereof.

Section 27. Officers and Employees Compensation.
The general assembly shall prescribe by law or by joint resolution the number, duties, and compensation of the appointed officers and employees of each house and of the two houses, and no payment shall be made from the state treasury, or be in any way authorized to any person except to an officer or employee appointed and acting pursuant to law or joint resolution.

Section 28. Extra Compensation to Officers, Employees, or Contractors Forbidden.
No bill shall be passed giving any extra compensation to any public officer or employee, agent, or contractor after services have been rendered or contract made nor providing for the payment of any claim made against the state without previous authority of law.

Section 29. Contracts for Facilities and Supplies.
All stationery, printing, paper, and fuel used in the legislative and other departments of government shall be furnished; and the printing and binding and distributing of the laws, journals, department reports, and other printing and binding; and the repairing and furnishing the halls and rooms used for the meeting of the general assembly and its committees, shall be performed under contract, to be given to the lowest responsible bidder, below such maximum price and under such regulations as may be prescribed by law. No member or officer of any department of the government shall be in any way interested in any such contract; and all such contracts shall be subject to the approval of the governor or his designee.

Section 30. Salary of Governor and Judges to Be Fixed by the Legislature Term Not to Be Extended or Salaries Increased or Decreased.

Repealed.

Section 31. Revenue Bills.
All bills for raising revenue shall originate in the house of representatives; but the senate may propose amendments, as in the case of other bills.

Section 32. Appropriation Bills.
The general appropriation bill shall embrace nothing but appropriations for the expense of the executive, legislative and judicial departments of the state, state institutions, interest on the public debt and for public schools. All other appropriations shall be made by separate bills, each embracing but one subject.

Section 33. Disbursement of Public Money.
No moneys in the state treasury shall be disbursed therefrom by the treasurer except upon appropriations made by law, or otherwise authorized by law, and any amount disbursed shall be substantiated by vouchers signed and approved in the manner prescribed by law.

Section 34. Appropriations to Private Institutions Forbidden.
No appropriation shall be made for charitable, industrial, educational or benevolent purposes to any person, corporation or community not under the absolute control of the state, nor to any denominational or sectarian institution or association.

Section 35. Delegation of Power.
The general assembly shall not delegate to any special commission, private corporation or association, any power to make, supervise or interfere with any municipal improvement, money, property or effects, whether held in trust or otherwise, or to levy taxes or perform any municipal function whatever.

Section 36. Laws on Investment of Trust Funds.
The general assembly shall, from time to time, enact laws prescribing types or classes of investments for the investment of funds held by executors, administrators, guardians, conservators and other trustees, whose power of investment is not set out in the instrument creating the trust.

Section 37. Change of Venue.

Repealed.

Section 38. No Liability Exchanged or Released.
No obligation or liability of any person, association, or corporation, held or owned by the state, or any municipal corporation therein, shall ever be exchanged, transferred, remitted, released, or postponed or in any way diminished by the general assembly, nor shall such liability or obligation be extinguished except by payment thereof into the proper treasury. This section shall not prohibit the write- off or release of uncollectible accounts as provided by general law.

Section 39. Orders and Resolutions Presented to Governor.
Every order, resolution or vote to which the concurrence of both houses may be necessary, except on the question of adjournment, or relating solely to the transaction of business of the two houses, shall be presented to the governor, and before it shall take effect, be approved by him, or being disapproved, shall

be re-passed by two-thirds of both houses, according to the rules and limitations prescribed in case of a bill.

Section 40. Bribery and Influence in General Assembly.

If any person elected to either house of the general assembly shall offer or promise to give his vote or influence in favor of or against any measure or proposition pending or proposed to be introduced in the general assembly in consideration or upon condition that any other person elected to the same general assembly will give or will promise or assent to give his vote or influence in favor of or against any other measure or proposition pending or proposed to be introduced in such general assembly, the person making such offer or promise, shall be deemed guilty of solicitation of bribery. If any member of the general assembly shall give his vote or influence for or against any measure or proposition pending in such general assembly, or offer, promise or assent so to do, upon condition that any other member will give or will promise or assent to give his vote or influence in favor of or against any other measure or proposition pending or proposed to be introduced in such general assembly, or in consideration that any other member hath given his vote or influence for or against any other measure or proposition in such general assembly, he shall be deemed guilty of bribery; and any member of the general assembly, or person elected thereto, who shall be guilty of either of such offenses shall be expelled, and shall not be thereafter eligible to the same general assembly; and, on conviction thereof in the civil courts, shall be liable to such further penalty as may be prescribed by law.

Section 41. Offering, Giving, Promising Money or Other Consideration.

Repealed.

Section 42. Corrupt Solicitation of Members and Officers.

Repealed.

Section 43. Member Interested Shall Not Vote.
A member who has a personal or private interest in any measure or bill proposed or pending before the general assembly, shall disclose the fact to the house of which he is a member, and shall not vote thereon.

Section 44. Representatives in Congress.
The general assembly shall divide the state into as many congressional districts as there are representatives in congress apportioned to the state by the congress of United States for the election of one representative to congress for each district. When a new apportionment shall be made by congress, the general assembly shall divide the state into congressional districts accordingly.

Section 45. General Assembly.
The general assembly shall consist of not more than thirty -five members of the senate and of not more than sixty- five members of the house of representatives, one to be elected from each senatorial and each representative district, respectively.

Section 46. Senatorial and Representative Districts.
The state shall be divided into as many senatorial and representative districts as there are members of the senate and house of representatives respectively, each district in each house having a population as nearly equal as may be, as required by the constitution of the United States, but in no event shall there be more than five percent deviation between the most populous and the least populous district in each house.

Section 47. Composition of Districts.

(1) Each district shall be as compact in area as possible and the aggregate linear distance of all district boundaries shall be as short as possible. Each district shall consist of contiguous whole general election precincts. Districts of the same house shall not overlap.

(2) Except when necessary to meet the equal population requirements of section 46, no part of one county shall be added to all or part of another county in forming districts. Within counties whose territory is contained in more than one district of the same house, the number of cities and towns whose territory is contained in more than one district of the same house shall be as small as possible. When county, city, or town boundaries are changed, adjustments, if any, in legislative districts shall be as prescribed by law.

(3) Consistent with the provisions of this section and section 46 of this article, communities of interest, including ethnic, cultural, economic, trade area, geographic, and demographic factors, shall be preserved within a single district wherever possible.

Section 48. Revision and Alteration of Districts Reapportionment Commission.

(1) (a) After each federal census of the United States, the senatorial districts and representative districts shall be established, revised, or altered, and the members of the senate and the house of representatives apportioned among them, by a Colorado reapportionment commission consisting of eleven members, to be appointed and having the qualifications as prescribed in this section. Of such members, four shall be appointed by the legislative department, three by the executive department, and four by the judicial department of the state.

(b) The four legislative members shall be the speaker of the house of representatives, the minority leader of the house of representatives, and the majority and minority leaders of the senate, or the designee of any such officer to serve in his stead, which acceptance of service or designation shall be made no later than July 1 of the year following that in which the federal census is taken. The three executive members shall be appointed by the governor between July 1 and July 10 of such year, and the four judicial members shall be appointed by the chief justice of the Colorado supreme court between July 10 and July 20 of such year.

(c) Commission members shall be qualified electors of the state of Colorado. No more than four commission members shall be members of the general assembly. No more than six commission members shall be affiliated with the same political party. No more than four commission members shall be residents of the same congressional district, and each congressional district shall have at least one resident as a commission member. At least one commission member shall reside west of the continental divide.

(d) Any vacancy created by the death or resignation of a member, or otherwise, shall be filled by the respective appointing authority. Members of the commission shall hold office until their reapportionment and redistricting plan is implemented. No later than August 1 of the year of their appointment, the governor shall convene the commission and appoint a temporary chairman who shall preside until the commission elects its own officers.

(e) Within ninety days after the commission has been convened or the necessary census data are available, whichever is later, the commission shall publish a preliminary plan for reapportionment of the members of the general assembly and shall hold public hearings thereon in several places throughout the state within forty-five days after the date of such publication. Within forty-five days after the completion of such hearings, the commission shall finalize its plan and submit the same to the Colorado supreme court for review and determination as to compliance with sections 46 and 47 of this article. Such review and determination shall take precedence over other matters before the court. The supreme court shall adopt rules for such proceedings and for the production and presentation of supportive evidence for such plan. The supreme court shall either approve the plan or return the plan and the court's reasons for disapproval to the commission. If the plan is returned, the commission shall revise and modify it to conform to the court's requirements and resubmit the plan to the court within twenty days. If the plan is approved by the court, it shall be filed with the secretary of state for implementation no later than March 15 of the second year following the year in which the census was taken. The commission shall keep a public record of all the proceedings of the commission and shall be responsible for the publication and distribution of copies of each plan.

(f) The general assembly shall appropriate sufficient funds for the compensation and payment of the expenses of the commission members and any staff employed by it. The commission shall have access to statistical information compiled by the state or its political subdivisions and necessary for its reapportionment duties.

Section 49. Appointment of State Auditor Term Qualifications Duties.

(1) The general assembly, by a majority vote of the members elected to and serving in each house, shall appoint, without regard to political affiliation, a state auditor, who shall be a certified public accountant licensed to practice in this state, to serve for a term of five years and until his successor is appointed and qualified. Except as provided by law, he shall be ineligible for appointment to any other public office in this state from which compensation is derived while serving as state auditor. He may be removed for cause at any time by a two-thirds vote of the members elected to and serving in each house.

(2) It shall be the duty of the state auditor to conduct post audits of all financial transactions and accounts kept by or for all departments, offices, agencies, and institutions of the state government, including educational institutions notwithstanding the provisions of section 14 of article IX of this constitution, and to perform similar or related duties with respect to such political subdivisions of the state as shall from time to time be required of him by law.

(3) Not more than three members of the staff of the state auditor shall be exempt from the personnel system of this state.

Section 50. Public Funding of Abortion Forbidden.
No public funds shall be used by the State of Colorado, its agencies or political subdivisions to pay or otherwise reimburse, either directly or indirectly, any person, agency or facility for the performance of any induced abortion, PROVIDED HOWEVER, that the General Assembly, by specific bill, may authorize and appropriate funds to be used for those medical services necessary to prevent the death of either a pregnant woman or her unborn child under circumstances where every reasonable effort is made to preserve the life of each.

Article VI: Judicial Department

Section 1. Vestment of Judicial Power
The judicial power of the state shall be vested in a supreme court, district courts, a probate court in the city and county of Denver, a juvenile court in the city and county of Denver, county courts, and such other courts or judicial officers with jurisdiction inferior to the supreme court, as the general assembly may, from time to time establish; provided, however, that nothing herein contained shall be construed to restrict or diminish the powers of home rule cities and towns granted under article XX, section 6 of this constitution to create municipal and police courts.

Supreme Court

Section 2. Appellate Jurisdiction

(1) The supreme court, except as otherwise provided in this constitution, shall have appellate jurisdiction only, which shall be coextensive with the state, and shall have a general superintending control over all inferior courts, under such regulations and limitations as may be prescribed by law.

(2) Appellate review by the supreme court of every final judgment of the district courts, the probate court of the city and county of Denver, and the juvenile court of the city and county of Denver shall be allowed, and the supreme court shall have such other appellate review as may be provided by law. There shall be no appellate review by the district court of any final judgment of the probate court of the city and county of Denver or of the juvenile court of the city and county of Denver.

Section 3. Original Jurisdiction -Opinions
The supreme court shall have power to issue writs of habeas corpus, mandamus, quo warranto, certiorari, injunction, and such other original and remedial writs as may be provided by rule of

court with authority to hear and determine the same; and each judge of the supreme court shall have like power and authority as to writs of habeas corpus. The supreme court shall give its opinion upon important questions upon solemn occasions when required by the governor, the senate, or the house of representatives; and all such opinions shall be published in connection with the reported decision of said court.

Section 4. Terms

At least two terms of the supreme court shall be held each year, at the seat of government.

Section 5. Personnel of Court -Departments -Chief Justice

(1) The supreme court shall consist of not less than seven justices, who may sit en banc or in departments. In case said court shall sit in departments, each of said departments shall have full power and authority of said court in the determination of causes, the issuing of writs and the exercise of all powers authorized by this constitution, or provided by law, subject to the general control of the court sitting en banc, and such rules and regulations as the court may make, but no decision of any department shall become judgment of the court unless concurred in by at least three justices, and no case involving construction of the constitution of this state or of the United States shall be decided except by the court en banc. Upon request of the supreme court, the number of justices may be increased to no more than nine members whenever two-thirds of the members of each house of the general assembly concur therein.

(2) The supreme court shall select a chief justice from its own membership to serve at the pleasure of a majority of the court, who shall be the executive head of the judicial system.

(3) The supreme court shall appoint a court administrator and such other personnel as the court may deem necessary to aid

the administration of the courts. Whenever the chief justice deems assignment of a judge necessary to the prompt disposition of judicial business, he may:
(a) Assign any county judge, or retired county judge who consents, temporarily to perform judicial duties in any county court if otherwise qualified under section 18 of this article, or assign, as hereafter may be authorized by law, said judge to any other court; or
(b) assign any district, probate, or juvenile judge, or retired justice or district, probate, or juvenile judge who consents, temporarily to perform judicial duties in any court. For each day of such temporary service a retired justice or judge shall receive compensation in an amount equal to 1/20 of the monthly salary then currently applicable to the judicial position in which the temporary service is rendered.

(4) The chief justice shall appoint from the district judges of each judicial district a chief judge to serve at the pleasure of the chief justice. A chief judge shall receive no additional salary by reason of holding such position. Each chief judge shall have and exercise such administrative powers over all judges of all courts within his district as may be delegated to him by the chief justice.

Section 6. Election of Judges

Repealed.

Section 7. Term of Office
The full term of office of justices of the supreme court shall be ten years.

Section 8. Qualifications of Justices
No person shall be eligible to the office of justice of the supreme court unless he shall be a qualified elector of the state of Colorado and shall have been licensed to practice law in this state for at least five years.

District Courts

Section 9. District Courts -Jurisdiction

(1) The district courts shall be trial courts of record with general jurisdiction, and shall have original jurisdiction in all civil, probate, and criminal cases, except as otherwise provided herein, and shall have such appellate jurisdiction as may be prescribed by law.

(2) Effective the second Tuesday in January, 1965, all causes pending before the county court in each county, except those causes within the jurisdiction of the county court as provided by law, and except as provided in subsection (3) of this section, shall then be transferred to and pending in the district court of such county, and no bond or obligation given in any of said causes shall be affected by said transfer.

(3) In the city and county of Denver, exclusive original jurisdiction in all matters of probate, settlements of estates of deceased persons, appointment of guardians, conservators and administrators, and settlement of their accounts, the adjudication of the mentally ill, and such other jurisdiction as may be provided by law shall be vested in a probate court, created by section 1 of this article, and to which court all of such jurisdiction of the county court of the city and county of Denver shall be transferred, including all pending cases and matters, effective on the second Tuesday of January, 1965.

Section 10. Judicial Districts -District Judges

(1) The state shall be divided into judicial districts. Such districts shall be formed of compact territory and be bounded by county lines. The judicial districts as provided by law on the effective date of this amendment shall constitute the judicial districts of the state until changed. The general assembly may by law, whenever two-thirds of the members of each house concur therein, change the boundaries of any district or increase or diminish the number of judicial districts.

(2) In each judicial district there shall be one or more judges of the district court. The full term of office of a district judge shall be six years.

(3) The number of district judges provided by law for each district on the effective date of this amendment shall constitute the number of judges for the district until changed. The general assembly may by law, whenever two-thirds of the members of each house concur therein, increase or diminish the number of district judges, except that the office of a district judge may not be abolished until completion of the term for which he was elected or appointed, but he may be required to serve in a judicial district other than the one for which elected, as long as such district encompasses his county of residence.

(4) Separate divisions of district courts may be established in districts by law, or in the absence of any such law, by rule of court.

Section 11. Qualifications of District Judges
No person shall be eligible to the office of district judge unless he shall be a qualified elector of the judicial district at the time of his election or selection and shall have been licensed to practice law in this state for five years. Each judge of the district court shall be a resident of his district during his term of office.

Section 12. Terms of Court
The time of holding courts within the judicial districts shall be as provided by rule of court, but at least one term of the district court shall be held annually in each

county.

District Attorneys

Section 13. District Attorneys -Election Term -Salary -Qualifications

In each judicial district there shall be a district attorney elected by the electors thereof, whose term of office shall be four years. District attorneys shall receive such salaries and perform such duties as provided by law. No person shall be eligible to the office of district attorney who shall not, at the time of his election possess all the qualifications of district court judges as provided in this article. All district attorneys holding office on the effective date of this amendment shall continue in office for the remainder of the respective terms for which they were elected or appointed.

Probates and Juvenile Courts

Section 14. Probate Court -Jurisdiction Judges -Election -Term -Qualifications

The probate court of the city and county of Denver shall have such jurisdiction as provided by section 9, subsection (3) of this article. The judge of the probate court of the city and county of Denver shall have the same qualifications and term of office as provided in this article for district judges and shall be elected initially by the qualified electors of the city and county of Denver at the general election in the year 1964. Vacancies shall be filled as provided in section 20 of this article. The number of judges of the probate court of the city and county of Denver may be increased as provided by law.

Section 15. Juvenile Court -Jurisdiction Judges -Election -Term -Qualifications

The juvenile court of the city and county of Denver shall have such jurisdiction as shall be provided by law. The judge of the juvenile court of the city and county of Denver shall have the same qualifications and term of office as provided in this article for district judges and shall be elected initially by the qualified electors of the city and county of Denver at the general election in the year 1964. Vacancies shall be filled as provided in section 20 of this article. The number of judges of the juvenile court of the city and county of Denver may be increased as provided by law.

County Courts

Section 16. County Judges -Terms -Qualifications
In each county there shall be one or more judges of the county court as may be provided by law, whose full term of office shall be four years, and whose qualifications shall be prescribed by law. County judges shall be qualified electors of their counties at the time of their election or appointment.

Section 17. County Courts -Jurisdiction -Appeals
County courts shall have such civil, criminal, and appellate jurisdiction as may be provided by law, provided such courts shall not have jurisdiction of felonies or in civil cases where the boundaries or title to real property shall be in question. Appellate review by the supreme court or the district courts of every final judgment of the county courts shall be as provided by law.

Miscellaneous

Section 18. Compensation and Services
Justices and judges of courts of record shall receive such compensation as may be provided by law, which may be increased but may not be decreased during their term of office and shall receive such pension or retirement benefits as may be provided by law. No justice or judge of a court of record shall accept designation or nomination for any public office other than judicial without first resigning from his judicial office, nor shall he hold at any other time any other public office during his term of office, nor hold office in any political party organization, nor contribute to or campaign for any political party or candidate for political office. No supreme court justice, judge of any intermediate appellate court, district court judge, probate judge,

or juvenile judge shall engage in the practice of law. Justices, district judges, probate judges, and juvenile judges when called upon to do so, may serve in any state court with full authority as provided by law. Any county judge may serve in any other county court, or serve, as hereinafter may be authorized by law, in any other court, if possessing the qualifications prescribed by law for a judge of such county court, or other court, or as a municipal judge or police magistrate as provided by law, or in the case of home rule cities as provided by charter and ordinances.

Section 19. Laws Relating to Courts -Uniform
All laws relating to state courts shall be general and of uniform operation throughout the state, and except as hereafter in this section specified the organization, jurisdiction, powers, proceedings, and practice of all courts of the same class, and the force and effect of the proceedings, judgments and decrees of such courts severally shall be uniform. County courts may be classified or graded as may be provided by law, and the organization, jurisdiction, powers, proceedings, and practice of county courts within the same class or grade, and the force and effect of the proceedings, judgments and decrees of county courts in the same class or grade shall be uniform; provided, however, that the organization and administration of the county court of the city and county of Denver shall be as provided in the charter and ordinances of the city and county of Denver.

Section 20. Vacancies
(1) A vacancy in any judicial office in any court of record shall be filled by appointment of the governor, from a list of three nominees for the supreme court and any intermediate appellate court, and from a list of two or three nominees for all other courts of record, such list to be certified to him by the supreme court nominating commission for a vacancy in the supreme court or a vacancy in any intermediate appellate court, and by the judicial district nominating commission for a vacancy in any other court in that district. In case of more than one vacancy in any such court, the list shall contain not less than two more

nominees than there are vacancies to be filled. The list shall be submitted by the nominating commission not later than thirty days after the death, retirement, tender of resignation, removal under section 23, failure of an incumbent to file a declaration under section 25, or certification of a negative majority vote on the question of retention in office under section 25 hereof. If the governor shall fail to make the appointment (or all of the appointments in case of multiple vacancies) from such list within fifteen days from the day it is submitted to him, the appointment (or the remaining appointments in case of multiple vacancies) shall be made by the chief justice of the supreme court from the same list within the next fifteen days. A justice or judge appointed under the provisions of this section shall hold office for a provisional term of two years and then until the second Tuesday in January following the next general election. A nominee shall be under the age of seventy-two years at the time his name is submitted to the governor.
(2) All justices and judges of courts of record holding office on the effective date of this constitutional amendment shall continue in office for the remainder of the respective terms for which they were elected or appointed. Retention in office thereafter shall be by election as prescribed in section 25.
(3) Other vacancies occurring in judicial offices shall be filled as now or hereafter provided by law.
(4)Vacancies occurring in the office of district attorney shall be filled by appointment of the governor. District attorneys appointed under the provisions of this section shall hold office until the next general election and until their successors elected thereat shall be duly qualified. Such successors shall be elected for the remainder of the unexpired term in which the vacancy was created.

Section 21. Rule-making Power
The supreme court shall make and promulgate rules governing the administration of all courts and shall make and promulgate rules governing practice and procedure in civil and criminal cases, except that the general assembly shall have the power to provide simplified procedures in county courts for claims not

exceeding five hundred dollars and for the trial of misdemeanors.

Section 22. Process -Prosecution -in Name of People
In all prosecutions for violations of the laws of Colorado, process shall run in the name of "The People of the State of Colorado;" all prosecutions shall be carried on in the name and by the authority of "The People of the State of Colorado," and conclude, "against the peace and dignity of the same."

Section 23. Retirement and Removal of Justices and Judges

(1) On attaining the age of seventy-two a justice or judge of a court of record shall retire and his judicial office shall be vacant, except as otherwise provided in section 20 (2).
(2) Whenever a justice or judge of any court of this state has been convicted in any court of this state or of the United States or of any state, of a felony or other offense involving moral turpitude, the supreme court shall, of its own motion or upon petition filed by any person, and upon finding that such a conviction was had, enter its order suspending said justice or judge from office until such time as said judgment of conviction becomes final, and the payment of salary of said justice or judge shall also be suspended from the date of such order. If said judgment of conviction becomes final, the supreme court shall enter its order removing said justice or judge from office and declaring his office vacant and his right to salary shall cease from the date of the order of suspension. If said judgment of conviction is reversed with directions to enter a judgment of acquittal or if reversed for a new trial which subsequently results in a judgment of dismissal or acquittal, the supreme court shall enter its order terminating the suspension of said justice or judge and said justice or judge shall be entitled to his salary for the period of suspension. A plea of guilty or nolo contendere to such a charge shall be equivalent to a final conviction for the purpose of this section.

(3) (a) There shall be a commission on judicial discipline. It shall consist of: Two judges of district courts and two judges of county courts, each selected by the supreme court; two citizens admitted to practice law in the courts of this state, neither of whom shall be a justice or judge, who shall have practiced in this state for at least ten years and who shall be appointed by the governor, with the consent of the senate; and four citizens, none of whom shall be a justice or judge, active or retired, nor admitted to practice law in the courts of this state, who shall be appointed by the governor, with the consent of the senate.
(b) Each member shall be appointed to a four-year term; except that one-half of the initial membership in each category shall be appointed to two-year terms, for the purpose of staggering terms. Whenever a commission membership prematurely terminates or a member no longer possesses the specific qualifications for the category from which he was selected, his position shall be deemed vacant, and his successor shall be appointed in the same manner as the original appointment for the remainder of his term. A member shall be deemed to have resigned if that member is absent from three consecutive commission meetings without the commission having entered an approval for additional absences upon its minutes. If any member of the commission is disqualified to act in any matter pending before the commission, the commission may appoint a special member to sit on the commission solely for the purpose of deciding that matter.
(c) No member of the commission shall receive any compensation for his services but shall be allowed his necessary expenses for travel, board, and lodging and any other expenses incurred in the performance of his duties, to be paid by the supreme court from its budget to be appropriated by the general assembly.
(d) A justice or judge of any court of record of this state, in accordance with the procedure set forth in this subsection (3), may be removed or disciplined for willful misconduct in office, willful or persistent failure to perform his duties, intemperance, or violation of any canon of the Colorado code of judicial conduct, or he may be retired for disability interfering with the

performance of his duties which is, or is likely to become, of a permanent character.

(e) The commission may, after such investigation as it deems necessary, order informal remedial action; order a formal hearing to be held before it concerning the removal, retirement, suspension, censure, reprimand, or other discipline of a justice or a judge; or request the supreme court to appoint three special masters, who shall be justices or judges of courts of record, to hear and take evidence in any such matter and to report thereon to the commission. After a formal hearing or after considering the record and report of the masters, if the commission finds good cause therefore, it may take informal remedial action, or it may recommend to the supreme court the removal, retirement, suspension, censure, reprimand, or discipline, as the case may be, of the justice or judge. The commission may also recommend that the costs of its investigation and hearing be assessed against such justice or judge.

(f) Following receipt of a recommendation from the commission, the supreme court shall review the record of the proceedings on the law and facts and in its discretion may permit the introduction of additional evidence and shall order removal, retirement, suspension, censure, reprimand, or discipline, as it finds just and proper, or wholly reject the recommendation. Upon an order for retirement, the justice or judge shall thereby be retired with the same rights and privileges as if he retired pursuant to statute. Upon an order for removal, the justice or judge shall thereby be removed from office, and his salary shall cease from the date of such order. On the entry of an order for retirement or for removal of a judge, his office shall be deemed vacant.

(g) Prior to the filing of a recommendation to the supreme court by the commission against any justice or judge, all papers filed with and proceedings before the commission on judicial discipline or masters appointed by the supreme court, pursuant to this subsection (3), shall be confidential, and the filing of papers with and the giving of testimony before the commission or the masters shall be privileged; but no other publication of such papers or proceedings shall be privileged in any action for defamation; except that the record filed by the commission in the supreme court continues privileged and a writing which was privileged prior to its filing with the commission or the masters does not lose such privilege by such filing.

(h) The supreme court shall by rule provide for procedures before the commission on judicial discipline, the masters, and the supreme court. The rules shall also provide the standards and degree of proof to be applied by the commission in its proceedings. A justice or judge who is a member of the commission or supreme court shall not participate in any proceedings involving his own removal or retirement.

(i) Nothing contained in this subsection (3) shall be construed to have any effect on article XIII of this constitution.

(j) Repealed.

Section 24. Judicial Nominating Commissions

(1) There shall be one judicial nominating commission for the supreme court and any intermediate appellate court to be called the supreme court nominating commission and one judicial nominating commission for each judicial district in the state.

(2) The supreme court nominating commission shall consist of the chief justice or acting chief justice of the supreme court, ex officio, who shall act as chairman and shall have no vote, one citizen admitted to practice law before the courts of this state and one other citizen not admitted to practice law in the courts of this state residing in each congressional district in the state, and one additional citizen not admitted to practice law in the courts of this state. No more than one-half of the commission members plus one, exclusive of the chief justice, shall be members of the same political party. Three voting members shall serve until December 31, 1967, three until December 31, 1969, and three until December 31, 1971. Thereafter each voting member appointed shall serve until the 31st of December of the 6th year following the date of his appointment.

(3) Each judicial district nominating commission shall consist of a justice of the supreme court designated by the chief justice, to serve at the will of the chief justice who shall act as chairman ex officio, and shall have no vote, and seven citizens residing in that judicial district, no more than four of whom shall be members of the same political party and there shall be at least one voting member from each county in the district. In all judicial districts having a population of more than 35,000 inhabitants as determined by the last preceding census taken under the authority of the United States, the voting members shall consist of three persons admitted to practice law in the courts of this state and four persons not admitted to practice law in the courts of this state. In judicial districts having a population of 35,000 inhabitants or less as determined above, at least four voting members shall be persons not admitted to practice law in the courts of this state; and it shall be determined by majority vote of the governor, the attorney general and the chief justice, how many, if any, of the remaining three members shall be persons admitted to practice law in the courts of this state. Two voting members shall serve until December 31, 1967, two until December 31, 1969, and three until December 31, 1971. Thereafter each voting member appointed shall serve until the 31st of December of the 6th year following the date of his appointment.

(4) Members of each judicial nominating commission selected by reason of their being citizens admitted to practice law in the courts of this state shall be appointed by majority action of the governor, the attorney general and the chief justice. All other members shall be appointed by the governor. No voting member of a judicial nominating commission shall hold any elective and salaried United States or state public office or any elective political party office and he shall not be eligible for reappointment to succeed himself on a commission. No voting member of the supreme court nominating commission shall be eligible for appointment as a justice of the supreme court or any intermediate appellate court so long as he is a member of that commission and for a period of three years thereafter; and no voting member of a judicial district nominating commission shall be eligible for appointment to judicial office in that district while a member of that commission and for a period of one year thereafter.

Section 25. Election of Justices and Judges

A justice of the supreme court or a judge of any other court of record, who shall desire to retain his judicial office for another term after the expiration of his then term of office shall file with the secretary of state, not more than six months nor less than three months prior to the general election next prior to the expiration of his then term of office, a declaration of his intent to run for another term. Failure to file such a declaration within the time specified shall create a vacancy in that office at the end of his then term of office. Upon the filing of such a declaration, a question shall be placed on the appropriate ballot at such general election, as follows:

"Shall Justice (Judge) .... of the Supreme (or other) Court be retained in office? YES/...../NO/...../." If a majority of those voting on the question vote "Yes," the justice or judge is thereupon elected to a succeeding full term. If a majority of those voting on the question vote "No," this will cause a vacancy to exist in that office at the end of his then present term of office.

In the case of a justice of the supreme court or any intermediate appellate court, the electors of the state at large; in the case of a judge of a district court, the electors of that judicial district; and in the case of a judge of the county court or other court of record, the electors of that county; shall vote on the question of retention in office of the justice or judge.

Section 26. Denver County Judges

The provisions of sections 16, 20, 23, 24 and 25 hereof shall not be applicable to judges of the county court of the City and County of Denver. The number, manner of selection, qualifications, term of office, tenure, and removal of such judges shall be as provided in the charter and ordinances of the City and County of Denver.

Article VII: Suffrage and Elections

Section 1. Qualifications of Elector.
Every citizen of the United States who has attained the age of eighteen years, has resided in this state for such time as may be prescribed by law, and has been duly registered as a voter if required by law shall be qualified to vote at all elections.
Section 1a. Qualifications of Elector Residence on Federal Land. Any other provision of this constitution with regard to "qualifications of electors" notwithstanding, every citizen of the United States who shall be otherwise qualified and shall have resided in this state not less than three months next preceding the election at which he offers to vote, and in the county or precinct such time as may be prescribed by law, shall be qualified to vote at all elections; provided, that the general assembly may by law extend to citizens of the United States who have resided in this state less than three months, the right to vote for presidential and vice- presidential electors, United States senators, and United States representatives.
Any person who otherwise meets the requirements of law for voting in this state shall not be denied the right to vote in an election because of residence on land situated within this state that is under the jurisdiction of the United States.

Section 2. Suffrage to Women.

Repealed.

Section 3. Educational Qualifications of Elector.

Deleted by amendment.

Section 4. When Residence Does Not Change.
For the purpose of voting and eligibility to office, no person shall be deemed to have gained a residence by reason of his presence, or lost it by reason of his absence, while in the civil or military service of the state, or of the United States, nor while a student at any institution of learning, nor while kept at public

expense in any poorhouse or other asylum, nor while confined in public prison.

Section 5. Privilege of Voters.
Voters shall in all cases, except treason, felony or breach of the peace, be privileged from arrest during their attendance at elections, and in going to and returning therefrom.

Section 6. Electors Only Eligible to Office.
No person except a qualified elector shall be elected or appointed to any civil or military office in the state.

Section 7 General Election.
The general election shall be held on such day as may be prescribed by law.

Section 8. Elections by Ballot or Voting Machine.
All elections by the people shall be by ballot, and in case paper ballots are required to be used, no ballots shall be marked in any way whereby the ballot can be identified as the ballot of the person casting it. The election officers shall be sworn or affirmed not to inquire or disclose how any elector shall have voted. In all cases of contested election in which paper ballots are required to be used, the ballots cast may be counted and compared with the list of voters, and examined under such safeguards and regulations as may be provided by law. Nothing in this section, however, shall be construed to prevent the use of any machine or mechanical contrivance for the purpose of receiving and registering the votes cast at any election, provided that secrecy in voting is preserved.

When the governing body of any county, city, city and county or town, including the city and county of Denver, and any city, city and county or town which may be governed by the provisions of special charter, shall adopt and purchase a voting machine, or voting machines, such governing body may provide for the payment therefore by the issuance of interest -bearing bonds, certificates of indebtedness or other obligations, which shall be a charge upon such city, city and county, or town; such bonds, certificates or other obligations may be made payable at such time or times, not exceeding ten years from date of issue, as may be determined, but shall not be issued or sold at less than par.

Section 9. No Privilege to Witness in Election Trial.
In trials of contested elections, and for offenses arising under the election law, no person shall be permitted to withhold his testimony on the ground that it may criminate himself, or subject him to public infamy; but such testimony shall not be used against him in any judicial proceeding, except for perjury in giving such testimony.

Section 10. Disfranchisement During Imprisonment.
No person while confined in any public prison shall be entitled to vote; but every such person who was a qualified elector prior to such imprisonment, and who is released therefrom by virtue of a pardon, or by virtue of having served out his full term of imprisonment, shall without further action, be invested with all the rights of citizenship, except as otherwise provided in this constitution.

Section 11. Purity of Elections.
The general assembly shall pass laws to secure the purity of elections, and guard against abuses of the elective franchise.

Section 12. Election Contests by Whom Tried.
The general assembly shall, by general law, designate the courts and judges by whom the several classes of election contests, not herein provided for, shall be tried, and regulate the manner of trial, and all matters incident thereto, but no such law shall apply to any contest arising out of an election held before its passage.

Article VIII: State Institutions

Section 1. Established and Supported by State.
Educational, reformatory and penal institutions, and those for the benefit of insane, blind, deaf and mute, and such other institutions as the public good may require, shall be established and supported by the state, in such manner as may be prescribed by law.

Section 2. Seat of Government Where Located.
The general assembly shall have no power to change or to locate the seat of government of the state, which shall remain at the city and county of Denver.

Section 3. Seat of Government - How Changed - Definitions

(1) When the seat of government shall have been located in the city and county of Denver as provided in section 2 of this article, the location thereof shall not thereafter be changed, except by a vote of two-thirds of all the qualified electors of the state voting on that question, at a general election, at which the question of location of the seat of government shall have been submitted by the general assembly.

(2) Notwithstanding the provisions of subsection (1) of this section, if the governor determines that a disaster emergency exists that substantially affects the ability of the state government to operate in the city and county of Denver, the governor may issue an executive order declaring a disaster emergency. After declaring the disaster emergency and after consulting with the chief justice of the supreme court, the president of the senate, and the speaker of the house of representatives, the governor may designate a temporary meeting location for the general assembly.

(3) After the declaration of a disaster emergency by the governor, the general assembly shall convene at the temporary meeting location, whether during regular session or in a special session convened by the governor or by written request by two-

thirds of the members of each house. The general assembly, acting by bill, may then designate a temporary location for the seat of government. The bill shall contain a date on which the temporary location of the seat of government shall expire.
(4) As used in this section:

(a) "Disaster emergency" means the occurrence or imminent threat of widespread or severe damage, injury, illness, or loss of life or property resulting from an epidemic or a natural, man-made, or technological cause.
(b) "Seat of government" means the location of the legislative, executive, and judicial branches of the state of Colorado.

Section 4. Appropriation for Capitol Building.

Repealed.

Section 5. Educational Institutions.

(1) The following educational institutions are declared to be state institutions of higher education: The university at Boulder, Colorado Springs, and Denver; the university at Fort Collins; the school of mines at Golden; and such other institutions of higher education as now exist or may hereafter be established by law if they are designated by law as state institutions. The establishment, management, and abolition of the state institutions shall be subject to the control of the state, under the provisions of the constitution and such laws and regulations as the general assembly may provide; except that the regents of the university at Boulder, Colorado Springs, and Denver may, whenever in their judgment the needs of that institution demand such action, establish, maintain, and conduct all or any part of the schools of medicine, dentistry, nursing, and pharmacy of the university, together with hospitals and supporting facilities and programs related to health, at Denver; and further, that nothing in this section shall be construed to prevent state educational institutions from giving temporary lecture courses in any part of the state, or conducting class excursions for the purpose of investigation and study; and provided further, that subject to prior approval by the general assembly, nothing in this section shall be construed to prevent the state institutions of higher education from hereafter establishing, maintaining, and conducting or discontinuing centers, medical centers, or branches of such institutions in any part of the state.

(2) The governing boards of the state institutions of higher education, whether established by this constitution or by law, shall have the general supervision of their respective institutions and the exclusive control and direction of all funds of and appropriations to their respective institutions, unless otherwise provided by law.

Article IX: Education

Section 1. Supervision of Schools Board of Education.
(1) The general supervision of the public schools of the state shall be vested in a board of education whose powers and duties shall be as now or hereafter prescribed by law. Said board shall consist of a member from each congressional district of the state and, if the total number of such congressional districts is an even number, one additional member, and said members shall be elected as hereinafter provided. The members of said board shall be elected by the registered electors of the state, voting at general elections, in such manner and for such terms as may be by law prescribed; provided, that provisions may be made by law for election of a member from each congressional district of the state by the electors of such district; and provided, further, that each member from a congressional district of the state shall be a qualified elector of such district. If the total number of congressional districts of the state is an even number, the additional member of said board shall be elected from the state at large. The members of said board shall serve without compensation, but they shall be reimbursed for any necessary expenses incurred by them in performing their duties as members of said board.

(2) The commissioner of education shall be appointed by the board of education and shall not be included in the classified civil service of the state.

(3) The qualifications, tenure, compensation, powers, and duties of said commissioner shall be as prescribed by law, subject to the supervision of said board.

Section 2. Establishment and Maintenance of Public Schools. The general assembly shall, as soon as practicable, provide for the establishment and maintenance of a thorough and uniform system of free public schools throughout the state, wherein all residents of the state, between the ages of six and twenty- one years, may be educated gratuitously. One or more public schools shall be maintained in each school district within the state, at least three months in each year; any school district failing to have such school shall not be entitled to receive any portion of the school fund for that year.

Section 3. School Fund Inviolate.
The public school fund of the state shall, except as provided in this article IX, forever remain inviolate and intact and the interest and other income thereon, only, shall be expended in the maintenance of the schools of the state, and shall be distributed amongst the several counties and school districts of the state, in such manner as may be prescribed by law. No part of this fund, principal, interest, or other income shall ever be transferred to any other fund, or used or appropriated, except as provided in this article IX. The state treasurer shall be the custodian of this fund, and the same shall be securely and profitably invested as may be by law directed. The state shall supply all losses thereof that may in any manner occur. In order to assist public schools in the state in providing necessary buildings, land, and equipment, the general assembly may adopt laws establishing the terms and conditions upon which the state treasurer may (1) invest the fund in bonds of school districts, (2) use all or any portion of the fund or the interest or other income thereon to guaranty bonds issued by school districts, or (3) make loans to school districts. Distributions of interest and other income for the benefit of public schools provided for in this article IX shall be in addition to and not a substitute for other moneys appropriated by the general assembly for such purposes.

Section 4. County Treasurer to Collect and Disburse.
Each county treasurer shall collect all school funds belonging to his county, and the several school districts therein, and disburse the same to the proper districts upon warrants drawn by the county superintendent, or by the proper district authorities, as may be provided by law.

Section 5. Of What School Fund Consists.
The public school fund of the state shall consist of the proceeds of such land as have heretofore been, or may hereafter, be granted to the state by the general government for educational purposes; all estates that may escheat to the state; also all other grants, gifts or devises that may be made to this state for educational purpose.

Section 6. County Superintendent of Schools.
There may be a county superintendent of schools in each county, whose term of office shall be four years, and whose duties, qualifications, and compensation shall be prescribed by law.
The provisions of section 8 of article XIV of this constitution to the contrary notwithstanding, the office of county superintendent of schools may be abolished by any county if the question of the abolishment of said office is first submitted, at a general election, to a vote of the qualified electors of said county and approved by a majority of the votes cast thereon. In any county so voting in favor of such abolishment, the office of county superintendent of schools and the term of office of any incumbent in said county shall terminate on June 30 following.
Amendments

Section 7. Aid to Private Schools, Churches, Sectarian Purpose, Forbidden.
Neither the general assembly, nor any county, city, town, township, school district or other public corporation, shall ever make any appropriation, or pay from any public fund or moneys whatever, anything in aid of any church or sectarian society, or for any sectarian purpose, or to help support or sustain any school, academy, seminary, college, university or other literary or scientific institution, controlled by any church or sectarian denomination whatsoever; nor shall any grant or donation of land, money or other personal property, ever be made by the state, or any such public corporation to any church, or for any sectarian purpose.

Section 8. Religious Test and Race Discrimination Forbidden Sectarian Tenets.

No religious test or qualification shall ever be required of any person as a condition of admission into any public educational institution of the state, either as a teacher or student; and no teacher or student of any such institution shall ever be required to attend or participate in any religious service whatsoever. No sectarian tenets or doctrines shall ever be taught in the public school, nor shall any distinction or classification of pupils be made on account of race or color, nor shall any pupil be assigned or transported to any public educational institution for the purpose of achieving racial balance.

Section 9. State Board of Land Commissioners.

(1) The state board of land commissioners shall be composed of five persons to be appointed by the governor, with the consent of the senate, one of whom shall be elected by the board as its president.

(2) The governor shall endeavor to appoint members of the board who reside in different geographic regions of the state. The board shall be composed of one person with substantial experience in production agriculture, one person with substantial experience in public primary or secondary education, one person with substantial experience in local government and land use planning, one person with substantial experience in natural resource conservation, and one citizen at large.

(3) The governor shall appoint a new board of land Commissioners on or before May 1, 1997. The term of each member shall be for four years; except that of the first board members appointed under this subsection (3), two members shall be appointed for terms that expire June 30, 1999, and three members shall be appointed for terms that expire June 30, 2001. The terms of office of the members of the board appointed prior to the effective date of this subsection (3) shall expire upon the confirmation of the first three members of the board appointed under this subsection (3). No member shall serve more than two consecutive terms. Members of the board shall be subject to removal, and vacancies of the board shall be filled, as provided in article IV, section 6 of this constitution.

(4) The board shall, pursuant to section 13 of article XII of this constitution, hire a director with the consent of the governor; and, through the director, a staff, and may contract for office space, acquire equipment and supplies, and enter into contracts as necessary to accomplish its duties. Payments for goods, services, and personnel shall be made from the income from the trusts lands. The general assembly shall annually appropriate from the income from the trusts lands, sufficient moneys to enable the board to perform its duties and in that regard shall give deference to the board's assessment of its budgetary needs. The members of the board shall not, by virtue of their appointment, be employees of the state, they may be reimbursed for their necessary and reasonable expenses and may, in addition, receive such per diem as may be established by the general assembly, from the income from trust lands.

(5) The individual members of the board shall have no personal liability for any action or failure to act as long as such action or failure to act does not involve willful for intentional malfeasance or gross negligence.

(6) The board shall serve as the trustee for the lands granted to the state in public trust by the federal government, lands acquired in lieu thereof, and additional lands held by the board in public trust. It shall have the duty to manage, control, and dispose of such lands in accordance with the purposes for which said grants of land were made and section 10 of this article IX, and subject to such terms and conditions consistent therewith as may be prescribed by law.

(7) The board shall have the authority to undertake nonsimultaneous exchanges of land, by directing that the proceeds from a particular sale or other disposition be deposited into a separate account to be established by the state treasurer with the interest thereon to accrue to such account, and withdrawing therefrom an equal or lesser amount to be used as the purchase price for the other land to be held and managed as provided in this article, provided that the purchase of lands to complete such an exchange shall be made within two years of the initial sale or disposition. Any proceeds, and the interest thereon, from a sale or other disposition which are not expended in completing the exchange shall be transferred by the state treasurer to the public school fund or such other trust fund maintained by the treasurer for the proceeds of the trust lands disposed of or sold. Moneys held in separate account shall not be used for the operating expenses of the board or for expenses incident to the disposition or acquisition of lands.

Section 10. Selection and Control of Public Lands.

(1) The state board of land commissioners shall be composed of five persons to be appointed by the governor, with the consent of the senate, one of whom shall be elected by the board as its president.
(2) The governor shall endeavor to appoint members of the board who reside in different geographic regions of the state. The board shall be composed of one person with substantial experience in production agriculture, one person with substantial experience in public primary or secondary education, one person with substantial experience in local government and land use planning, one person with substantial experience in natural resource conservation, and one citizen at large.
(3) The governor shall appoint a new board of land commissioners on or before May 1, 1997. The term of each member shall be for four years; except that of the first board members appointed under this subsection (3), two members shall be appointed for terms that expire June 30, 1999, and three members shall be appointed for terms that expire June 30, 2001. No member shall serve more than two consecutive terms. Members of the board shall be subject to removal, and vacancies on the board shall be filled, as provided in article IV, section 6 of this constitution.
(4) The board shall, pursuant to section 13 of article XII of this constitution, hire a director with the consent of the governor, and, through the director, a staff, and may contract for office space, acquire equipment and supplies, and enter into contracts as necessary to accomplish its duties. Payment for goods,

services, and personnel shall be made from the income from the trust lands. The general assembly shall annually appropriate from the income from the trust lands, sufficient moneys to enable the board to perform its duties and in that regard shall give deference to the board's assessment of its budgetary needs. The members of the board shall not, by virtue of their appointment, be employees of the state; they may be reimbursed for their reasonable and necessary expenses and may, in addition, receive such per diem as may be established by the general assembly, from the income from the trust lands.

(5) The individual members of the board shall have no personal liability for any action or failure to act as long as such action or failure to act does not involve willful or intentional malfeasance or gross negligence.

(6) The board shall serve as the trustee for the lands granted to the state in public trust by the federal government, lands acquired in lieu thereof, and additional lands held by the board in public trust. It shall have the duty to manage, control, and dispose of such lands in accordance with the purposes for which said grants of land were made and section 10 of this article IX, and subject to such terms and conditions consistent therewith as may be prescribed by law.

(7) The board shall have the authority to undertake nonsimultaneous exchanges of land, by directing that the proceeds from a particular sale or other disposition be deposited into a separate account to be established by the state treasurer with the interest thereon to accrue to such account, and withdrawing therefrom an equal or lesser amount to be used as the purchase price for other land to be held and managed as provided in this article, provided that the purchase of lands to complete such an exchange shall be made within two years of the initial sale or disposition. Any proceeds, and the interest thereon, from a sale or other disposition which are not expended in completing the exchange shall be transferred by the state treasurer to the public school fund or such other trust fund maintained by the treasurer for the proceeds of the trust lands disposed of or sold. Moneys held in the separate account shall not be used for the operating expenses of the board or for

expenses incident to the disposition or acquisition of lands.
Amendments

Section 11. Compulsory Education.
The general assembly may require, by law, that every child of sufficient mental and physical ability, shall attend the public school during the period between the ages of six and eighteen years, for a time equivalent to three years, unless educated by other means.

Section 12. Regents of University.
There shall be nine regents of the university of Colorado who shall be elected in the manner prescribed by law for terms of six years each. Said regents shall constitute a body corporate to be known by the name and style of "The Regents of the University of Colorado."The board of regents shall select from among its members a chairman who shall conduct the meetings of the board and a vice-chairman who shall assume the duties of the chairman in case of his absence.

Section 13. President of University.
The regents of the university shall elect a president of the university who shall hold his office until removed by the board of regents. He shall be the principal executive officer of the university, a member of the faculty thereof, and shall carry out the policies and programs established by the board of regents.

Section 14. Control of University.

Repealed.

Section 15. School Districts Board of Education.
The general assembly shall, by law, provide for organization of school districts of convenient size, in each of which shall be established a board of education, to consist of three or more directors to be elected by the qualified electors of the district. Said directors shall have control of instruction in the public schools of their respective districts.

Section 16. Textbooks in Public Schools.
Neither the general assembly nor the state board of education shall have power to prescribe textbooks to be used in the public schools.

Section 17. Education - Funding.

(1) PURPOSE. In state fiscal year 2001-2002 through state fiscal year 2010-2011, the statewide base per pupil funding, as defined by the Public School Finance Act of 1994, article 54 of title 22, Colorado Revised Statutes on the effective date of this section, for public education from preschool through the twelfth grade and total state funding for all categorical programs shall grow annually at least by the rate of inflation plus an additional one percentage point. In state fiscal year 2011-2012, and each fiscal year thereafter, the statewide base per pupil funding for public education from preschool through the twelfth grade and total state funding for all categorical programs shall grow annually at a rate set by the general assembly that is at least equal to the rate of inflation.

(2) DEFINITIONS. For purposes of this section: (a) "Categorical programs" include transportation programs, English language proficiency programs, expelled and at-risk student programs, special education programs (including gifted and talented programs), suspended student programs, vocational education programs, small attendance centers, comprehensive health education programs, and other current and future accountable programs specifically identified in statute as a categorical program.

(b) "Inflation" has the same meaning as defined in article X, section 20, subsection (2), paragraph (f) of the Colorado constitution.

(3) IMPLEMENTATION. In state fiscal year 2001-2002 and each fiscal year thereafter, the general assembly may annually appropriate, and school districts may annually expend, monies from the state education fund created in subsection (4) of this section. Such appropriations and expenditures shall not be subject to the statutory limitation on general fund appropriations growth, the limitation on fiscal year spending set forth in article X, section 20 of the Colorado constitution, or any other spending limitation existing in law.

(4) STATE EDUCATION FUND CREATED. (a) There is hereby created in the department of the treasury the state education fund. Beginning on the effective date of this measure, all state revenues collected from a tax of one third of one percent on federal taxable income, as modified by law, of every individual, estate, trust and corporation, as defined in law, shall be deposited in the state education fund. Revenues generated from a tax of one third of one percent on federaltaxable income, as modified by law, of every individual, estate, trust and corporation, as defined in law, shall not be subject to the limitation on fiscal year spending set forth in article X, section 20 of the Colorado constitution. All interest earned on monies in the state education fund shall be deposited in the state education fund and shall be used before any principal is depleted. Monies remaining in the state education fund at the end of any fiscal year shall remain in the fund and not revert to the general fund.

(b) In state fiscal year 2001-2002, and each fiscal year thereafter, the general assembly may annually appropriate monies from the state education fund. Monies in the state education fund may only be used to comply with subsection (1) of this section and for accountable education reform, for accountable programs to meet state academic standards, for class size reduction, for expanding technology education, for improving student safety, for expanding the availability of preschool and kindergarten programs, for performance incentives for teachers, for accountability reporting, or for public school building capital construction.

(5) MAINTENANCE OF EFFORT. Monies appropriated from the state education fund shall not be used to supplant the level of general fund appropriations existing on the effective date of this section for total program education funding under the Public

School Finance Act of 1994, article 54 of title 22, Colorado Revised Statutes, and for categorical programs as defined in subsection (2) of this section. In state fiscal year 2001-2002 through state fiscal year 2010-2011, the general assembly shall, at a minimum, annually increase the general fund appropriation for total program under the "Public School Finance Act of 1994," or any successor act, by an amount not below five percent of the prior year general fund appropriation for total program under the "Public School Finance Act of 1994," or any successor act. This general fund growth requirement shall not apply in any fiscal year in which Colorado personal income grows less than four and one half percent between the two previous calendar years.

Article X: Revenue

Section 1. Fiscal Year
The fiscal year shall commence on the first day of October in each year, unless otherwise provided by law.

Section 2. Tax Provided for State Expenses
The general assembly shall provide by law for an annual tax sufficient, with other resources, to defray the estimated expenses of the state government for each fiscal year.

Section 3. Uniform Taxation -Exemptions
(1)(a) Each property tax levy shall be uniform upon all real and personal property not exempt from taxation under this article located within the territorial limits of the authority levying the tax. The actual value of all real and personal property not exempt from taxation under this article shall be determined under general laws, which shall prescribe such methods and regulations as shall secure just and equalized valuations for assessments of all real and personal property not exempt from taxation under this article. Valuations for assessment shall be based on appraisals by assessing officers to determine the actual value of property in accordance with provisions of law, which laws shall provide that actual value be determined by appropriate consideration of cost approach, market approach, and income approach to appraisal. However, the actual value of residential real property shall be determined solely by consideration of cost approach and market approach to appraisal; and, however, the actual value of agricultural lands, as defined by law, shall be determined solely by consideration of the earning or productive capacity of such lands capitalized at a rate as prescribed by law.
(b) Residential real property, which shall include all residential dwelling units and the land, as defined by law, on which such units are located, and mobile home parks, but shall not include hotels and motels, shall be valued for assessment at twenty-one percent of its actual value. For the property tax year commencing January 1, 1985, the general assembly shall determine the percentage of the aggregate statewide valuation for assessment

which is attributable to residential real property. For each subsequent year, the general assembly shall again determine the percentage of the aggregate statewide valuation for assessment which is attributable to each class of taxable property, after adding in the increased valuation for assessment attributable to new construction and to increased volume of mineral and oil and gas production. For each year in which there is a change in the level of value used in determining actual value, the general assembly shall adjust the ratio of valuation for assessment for residential real property which is set forth in this paragraph (b) as is necessary to insure that the percentage of the aggregate statewide valuation for assessment which is attributable to residential real property shall remain the same as it was in the year immediately preceding the year in which such change occurs. Such adjusted ratio shall be the ratio of valuation for assessment for residential real property for those years for which such new level of value is used. In determining the adjustment to be made in the ratio of valuation for assessment for residential real property, the aggregate statewide valuation for assessment that is attributable to residential real property shall be calculated as if the full actual value of all owner-occupied primary residences that are partially exempt from taxation pursuant to section 3.5 of this article was subject to taxation. All other taxable property shall be valued for assessment at twenty-nine percent of its actual value. However, the valuation for assessment for producing mines, as defined by law, and lands or leaseholds producing oil or gas, as defined by law, shall be a portion of the actual annual or actual average annual production therefrom, based upon the value of the unprocessed material, according to procedures prescribed by law for different types of minerals. Non-producing unpatented mining claims, which are possessory interests in real property by virtue of leases from the United States of America, shall be exempt from property taxation.

(c) The following classes of personal property, as defined by law, shall be exempt from property taxation: Household furnishings and personal effects which are not used for the production of income at any time; inventories of merchandise and materials and supplies which are held for consumption by a business or are held primarily for sale; livestock; agricultural and livestock products; and agricultural equipment which is used on the farm or ranch in the production of agricultural products.

(d) Ditches, canals, and flumes owned and used by individuals or corporations for irrigating land owned by such individuals or corporations, or the individual members thereof, shall not be separately taxed so long as they shall be owned and used exclusively for such purposes.

(2)(a) During each property tax year beginning with the property tax year which commences January 1, 1983, the general assembly shall cause a valuation for assessment study to be conducted. Such study shall determine whether or not the assessor of each county has complied with the property tax provisions of this constitution and of the statutes in valuing property and has determined the actual value and valuation for assessment of each and every class of taxable real and personal property consistent with such provisions. Such study shall sample at least one percent of each and every class of taxable real and personal property in the county.

(b)(I) If the study conducted during the property tax year which commences January 1, 1983, shows that a county assessor did not comply with the property tax provisions of this constitution or the statutes or did not determine the actual value or the valuation for assessment of any class or classes of taxable real and personal property consistent with such provisions, the state board of equalization shall, during such year, order such county assessor to reappraise during the property tax year which commences January 1, 1984, such class or classes for such year. Such reappraisal shall be performed at the expense of the county.

(II) If the study performed during the property tax year which commences January 1, 1984, shows that the county assessor failed to reappraise such class or classes as ordered or failed in his reappraisal to meet the objections of the state board of equalization, the state board of equalization shall cause a reappraisal of such class or classes to be performed in the property tax year which commences January 1, 1985. The cost of such reappraisal shall be paid by the state by an appropriation authorized by law. However, if such reappraisal shows that the county assessor did not value or assess taxable property as prescribed by the provisions of this constitution or of the statutes, upon certification to the board of county commissioners by the state board of equalization of the cost thereof, the board of county commissioners shall pay to the state the cost of such reappraisal.

(III) The reappraisal performed in the property tax year which commences January 1, 1985, shall become the county's abstract for assessment with regard to such reappraised class or classes for such year. The state board of equalization shall order the county's board of county commissioners to levy, and the board of county commissioners shall levy, in 1985 an additional property tax on all taxable property in the county in an amount sufficient to repay, and the board of county commissioners shall repay, the state for any excess payment made by the state to school districts within the county during the property tax year which commences January 1, 1985.

(c)(I) Beginning with the property tax year which commences January 1, 1985, and applicable to each property tax year thereafter, the annual study conducted pursuant to paragraph (a) of this subsection (2) shall, in addition to the requirements set forth in paragraph (a) of this subsection (2), set forth the aggregate valuation for assessment of each county for the year in which the study is conducted.

(II) If the valuation for assessment of a county as reflected in its abstract for assessment is more than five percent below the valuation for assessment for such county as determined by the study, during the next following year, the state board of equalization shall cause to be performed, at the expense of the county, a reappraisal of any class or classes of taxable property which the study shows were not appraised consistent with the property tax provisions of this constitution or the statutes. The state board of equalization shall cause to be performed during the next following year, at the expense of the county, a reappraisal of any class or classes of taxable property which the study shows were not appraised consistent with the property tax provisions of this constitution or the statutes even though the county's aggregate valuation for assessment as reflected in the county's abstract for assessment was not more than five percent below the county's aggregate valuation for assessment as determined by the study. The reappraisal shall become the county's valuation for assessment with regard to such reappraised class or classes for the year in which the reappraisal was performed.

(III) In any case in which a reappraisal is ordered, state equalization payments to school districts within the county during the year in which the reappraisal is performed shall be based upon the valuation for assessment as reflected in the county's abstract for assessment. The state board of equalization shall also order the board of county commissioners of the county to impose, and the board of county commissioners shall impose, at the time of imposition of property taxes during such year an additional property tax on all taxable property within the county in an amount sufficient to repay, and the board of county commissioners shall repay, the state for any excess payments made by the state to school districts within the county during the year in which such reappraisal was performed plus interest thereon at a rate and for such time as are prescribed by law.

(IV) If the valuation for assessment of a county as reflected in its abstract for assessment is more than five percent below the valuation for assessment for such county as determined by the study and if the state board of equalization fails to order a reappraisal, state equalization payments to school districts within the county during the year following the year in which the study was conducted shall be based upon the valuation for assessment for the county as reflected in the county's abstract for assessment. The board of county commissioners of such county shall impose in the year in which such school payments are made an additional property tax on all taxable property in the county in an amount sufficient to repay, and the board of county commissioners shall repay, the state for the difference between the amount the state actually paid in state equalization payments during such year and what the state would have paid during such year had such state payments been based on the valuation for assessment as determined by the study.

Section 3.5 **Homestead exemption for qualifying senior citizens and disabled veterans**

(1) For property tax years commencing on or after January 1, 2002, fifty percent of the first two hundred thousand dollars of actual value of residential real property, as defined by law, that, as of the assessment date, is owner-occupied and is used as the primary residence of the owner-occupier shall be exempt from property taxation if:

(a) The owner-occupier is sixty-five years of age or older as of the assessment date and has owned and occupied such residential real property as his or her primary residence for the ten years immediately preceding the assessment date;
(b) The owner-occupier is the spouse or surviving spouse of an owner-occupier who previously qualified for a property tax exemption for the same residential real property under paragraph **(a)** of this subsection (1); or
(c) For property tax years commencing on or after January 1, 2007, only, the owner-occupier, as of the assessment date, is a disabled veteran.

(1.3) An owner-occupier may claim only one exemption per property tax year even if the owner-occupier qualifies for an exemption under both paragraph (c) of subsection (1) of this section and either paragraph (a) or paragraph (b) of subsection (1) of this section.
(1.5) For purposes of this section, "disabled veteran" means an individual who has served on active duty in the United States armed forces, including a member of the Colorado national guard who has been ordered into the active military service of the United States, has been separated therefrom under honorable conditions, and has established a service-connected disability that has been rated by the federal department of veterans affairs

as one hundred percent permanent disability through disability retirement benefits or a pension pursuant to a law or regulation administered by the department, the department of homeland security, or the department of the army, navy, or air force.
(2) Notwithstanding the provisions of subsection (1) of this section, section 20 of this article, or any other constitutional provision, for any property tax year commencing on or after January 1, 2003, the general assembly may raise or lower by law the maximum amount of actual value of residential real property of which fifty percent shall be exempt under subsection (1) of this section.
(3) For any property tax year commencing on or after January 1, 2002, the general assembly shall compensate each local governmental entity that receives property tax revenues for the net amount of property tax revenues lost as a result of the property tax exemption provided for in this section. For purposes of section 20 of article X of this constitution, such compensation shall not be included in local government fiscal year spending and approval of this section by the voters statewide shall constitute a voter-approved revenue change to allow the maximum amount of state fiscal year spending for the 2001-02 state fiscal year to be increased by forty-four million one hundred twenty-three thousand six hundred four dollars and to include said amount in state fiscal year spending for said state fiscal year for the purpose of calculating subsequent state fiscal year spending limits. Payments made from the state general fund to compensate local governmental entities for property tax revenues lost as a result of the property tax exemption provided for in this section shall not be subject to any statutory limitation on general fund appropriations because the enactment of this section by the people of Colorado constitutes voter approval of a weakening of any such limitation.

Section 4. Public Property Exempt
The property, real and personal, of the state, counties, cities, towns and other municipal corporations and public libraries, shall be exempt from taxation.

Section 5. Property Used for Religious Worship, Schools and Charitable Purposes Exempt

Property, real and personal, that is used solely and exclusively for religious worship, for schools or for strictly charitable purposes, also cemeteries not used or held for private or corporate profit, shall be exempt from taxation, unless otherwise provided by general law.

Section 6. Self-propelled Equipment, Motor Vehicles, and Certain Other Movable Equipment

The general assembly shall enact laws classifying motor vehicles and also wheeled trailers, semi-trailers, trailer coaches, and mobile and self-propelled construction equipment, prescribing methods of determining the taxable value of such property, and requiring payment of a graduated annual specific ownership tax thereon, which tax shall be in lieu of all ad valorem taxes upon such property; except that such laws shall not exempt from ad valorem taxation any such property in process of manufacture or held in storage, or which constitutes the inventory of manufacturers or distributors thereof or dealers therein; and further except that the general assembly shall provide by law for the taxation of mobile homes.

Such graduated annual specific ownership tax shall be in addition to any state registration or license fees imposed on such property, shall be payable to a designated county officer at the same time as any such registration or license fees are payable, and shall be apportioned, distributed, and paid over to the political subdivisions of the state in such manner as may be prescribed by law.

All laws exempting from taxation property other than that specified in this article shall be void.

Section 7. Municipal Taxation by General Assembly Prohibited

The general assembly shall not impose taxes for the purposes of any county, city, town or other municipal corporation, but may by law, vest in the corporate authorities thereof respectively, the power to assess and collect taxes for all purposes of such corporation.

Section 8. No County, City, Town to Be Released
No county, city, town or other municipal corporation, the inhabitants thereof, nor the property therein, shall be released or discharged from their or its proportionate share of taxes to be levied for state purposes.

Section 9. Relinquishment of Power to Tax Corporations Forbidden
The power to tax corporations and corporate property, real and personal, shall never be relinquished or suspended.

Section 10. Corporations Subject to Tax
All corporations in this state, or doing business therein, shall be subject to taxation for state, county, school, municipal and other purposes, on the real and personal property owned or used by them within the territorial limits of the authority levying the tax.

Section 11. Maximum Rate of Taxation
The rate of taxation on property, for state purposes, shall never exceed four mills on each dollar of valuation; provided, however, that in the discretion of the general assembly an additional levy of not to exceed one mill on each dollar of valuation may from time to time be authorized for the erection of additional buildings at, and for the use, benefit, maintenance, and support of the state educational institutions; provided, further, that the rate of taxation on property for all state purposes, including the additional levy herein provided for, shall never exceed five mills on each dollar of valuation, unless otherwise provided in the constitution.

Section 12. Public Funds -Report of State Treasurer

(1) The general assembly may provide by law for the safekeeping and management of the public funds in the custody of the state treasurer, but, notwithstanding any such provision, the state treasurer and his sureties shall be responsible therefore.

(2) The state treasurer shall keep adequate records of all moneys coming into his custody and shall at the end of each quarter of the fiscal year submit a written report to the governor, signed under oath, showing the condition of the state treasury, the amount of money in the several funds, and where such money is kept or deposited. Swearing falsely to any such report shall be deemed perjury.

(3) The governor shall cause every such quarterly report to be promptly published in at least one newspaper printed at the seat of government, and otherwise as the general assembly may require.

Section 13. Making Profit on Public Money -Felony

The making of profit, directly or indirectly, out of state, county, city, town or school district money, or using the same for any purpose not authorized by law, by any public officer, shall be deemed a felony, and shall be punished as provided by law.

Section 14. Private Property Not Taken for Public Debt

Private property shall not be taken or sold for the payment of the corporate debt of municipal corporations.

Section 15. Boards of Equalization -Duties Property Tax Administrator

(1)(a) There shall be in each county of the state a county board of equalization, consisting of the board of county commissioners of said county. As may be prescribed by law, the county boards of equalization shall raise, lower, adjust, and equalize valuations for assessment of taxes upon real and personal property located within their respective counties, subject to review and revision by the state board of equalization.

(b) There shall be a state board of equalization, consisting of the governor or his designee, the speaker of the house of representatives or his designee, the president of the senate or his designee, and two members appointed by the governor with the consent of the senate. Each of such appointed members shall be a qualified appraiser or a former county assessor or a person who has knowledge and experience in property taxation. The

general assembly shall provide by law for the political composition of such board and for the compensation of its members and, with regard to the appointed members, for terms of office, the filling of vacancies, and removal from office. As may be prescribed by law, the state board of equalization shall review the valuations determined for assessment of taxes upon the various classes of real and personal property located in the several counties of the state and shall, upon a majority vote, raise, lower, and adjust the same to the end that all valuations for assessment of taxes shall be just and equalized; except that said state board of equalization shall have no power of original assessment. Whenever a majority vote of the state board of equalization is prescribed by this constitution or by statute, "majority vote" means an affirmative vote of the majority of the entire membership of such board.
(c) The state board of equalization and the county boards of equalization shall perform such other duties as may be prescribed by law.

(2) The state board of equalization shall appoint, by a majority vote, a property tax administrator who shall serve for a term of five years and until his successor is appointed and qualified unless removed for cause by a majority vote of the state board of equalization. The property tax administrator shall have the duty, as provided by law, of administering the property tax laws and such other duties as may be prescribed by law and shall be subject to the supervision and control of the state board of equalization. The position of property tax administrator shall be exempt from the personnel system of this state.

Section 16. Appropriations Not to Exceed Tax -Exceptions
No appropriation shall be made, nor any expenditure authorized by the general assembly, whereby the expenditure of the state, during any fiscal year, shall exceed the total tax then provided for by law and applicable for such appropriation or expenditure, unless the general assembly making such appropriation shall provide for levying a sufficient tax, not exceeding the rates allowed in section eleven of this article, to pay such appropriation

or expenditure within such fiscal year. This provision shall not apply to appropriations or expenditures to suppress insurrection, defend the state, or assist in defending the United States in time of war.

Section 17. Income Tax
The general assembly may levy income taxes, either graduated or proportional, or both graduated and proportional, for the support of the state, or any political subdivision thereof, or for public schools, and may, in the administration of an income tax law, provide for special classified or limited taxation or the exemption of tangible and intangible personal property.

Section 18. License Fees and Excise Taxes -Use of
On and after July 1, 1935, the proceeds from the imposition of any license, registration fee, or other charge with respect to the operation of any motor vehicle upon any public highway in this state and the proceeds from the imposition of any excise tax on gasoline or other liquid motor fuel except aviation fuel used for aviation purposes shall, except costs of administration, be used exclusively for the construction, maintenance, and supervision of the public highways of this state. Any taxes imposed upon aviation fuel shall be used exclusively for aviation purposes.

Section 19. State Income Tax Laws by Reference to United States Tax Laws
The general assembly may by law define the income upon which income taxes may be levied under section 17 of this article by reference to provisions of the laws of the United States in effect from time to time, whether retrospective or prospective in their operation, and shall in any such law provide the dollar amount of personal exemptions to be allowed to the taxpayer as a deduction. The general assembly may in any such law provide for other exceptions or modifications to any of such provisions of the laws of the United States and for retrospective exceptions or modifications to those provisions which are retrospective.

Section 20. The Taxpayer's Bill of Rights

(1) General provisions. This section takes effect December 31, 1992 or as stated. Its preferred interpretation shall reasonably restrain most the growth of government. All provisions are self-executing and severable and supersede conflicting state constitutional, state statutory, charter, or other state or local provisions. Other limits on district revenue, spending, and debt may be weakened only by future voter approval. Individual or class action enforcement suits may be filed and shall have the highest civil priority of resolution. Successful plaintiffs are allowed costs and reasonable attorney fees, but a district is not unless a suit against it be ruled frivolous. Revenue collected, kept, or spent illegally since four full fiscal years before a suit is filed shall be refunded with 10% annual simple interest from the initial conduct. Subject to judicial review, districts may use any reasonable method for refunds under this section, including temporary tax credits or rate reductions. Refunds need not be proportional when prior payments are impractical to identify or return. When annual district revenue is less than annual payments on general obligation bonds, pensions, and final court judgments, (4) (a) and (7) shall be suspended to provide for the deficiency.

(2) Term definitions. Within this section:

(a) "Ballot issue" means a non-recall petition or referred measure in an election.
(b) "District" means the state or any local government, excluding enterprises.
(c) "Emergency" excludes economic conditions, revenue shortfalls, or district salary or fringe benefit increases.
(d) "Enterprise" means a government-owned business authorized to issue its own revenue bonds and receiving under 10% of annual revenue in grants from all Colorado state and local governments combined.
(e) "Fiscal year spending" means all district expenditures and reserve increases except, as to both, those for refunds made in the current or next fiscal year or those from gifts, federal funds,

collections for another government, pension contributions by employees and pension fund earnings, reserve transfers or expenditures, damage awards, or property sales.
(f) "Inflation" means the percentage change in the United States Bureau of Labor Statistics Consumer Price Index for Denver-Boulder, all items, all urban consumers, or its successor index.
(g) "Local growth" for a non-school district means a net percentage change in actual value of all real property in a district from construction of taxable real property improvements, minus destruction of similar improvements, and additions to, minus deletions from, taxable real property. For a school district, it means the percentage change in its student enrollment.

(3) Election provisions:

(a) Ballot issues shall be decided in a state general election, biennial local district election, or on the first Tuesday in November of odd-numbered years. Except for petitions, bonded debt, or charter or constitutional provisions, districts may consolidate ballot issues and voters may approve a delay of up to four years in voting on ballot issues. District actions taken during such a delay shall not extend beyond that period.
(b) At least 30 days before a ballot issue election, districts shall mail at the least cost, and as a package where districts with ballot issues overlap, a titled notice or set of notices addressed to "All Registered Voters" at each address of one or more active registered electors. The districts may coordinate the mailing required by this paragraph (b) with the distribution of the ballot information booklet required by section 1 (7.5) of article V of this constitution in order to save mailing costs. Titles shall have this order of preference: "NOTICE OF ELECTION TO INCREASE TAXES/TO INCREASE DEBT/ON A CITIZEN PETITION/ON A REFERRED MEASURE." Except for district voter-approved additions, notices shall include only:

(i) The election date, hours, ballot title, text, and local election office address and telephone number.

(ii) For proposed district tax or bonded debt increases, the estimated or actual total of district fiscal year spending for the current year and each of the past four years, and the overall percentage and dollar change.

(iii) For the first full fiscal year of each proposed district tax increase, district estimates of the maximum dollar amount of each increase and of district fiscal year spending without the increase.

(iv) For proposed district bonded debt, its principal amount and maximum annual and total district repayment cost, and the principal balance of total current district bonded debt and its maximum annual and remaining total district repayment cost.

(v) Two summaries, up to 500 words each, one for and one against the proposal, of written comments filed with the election officer by 45 days before the election. No summary shall mention names of persons or private groups, nor any endorsements of or resolutions against the proposal. Petition representatives following these rules shall write this summary for their petition. The election officer shall maintain and accurately summarize all other relevant written comments. The provisions of this subparagraph (v) do not apply to a statewide ballot issue, which is subject to the provisions of section 1 (7.5) of article V of this constitution.

(c) Except by later voter approval, if a tax increase or fiscal year spending exceeds any estimate in (b) (iii) for the same fiscal year, the tax increase is thereafter reduced up to 100% in proportion to the combined dollar excess, and the combined excess revenue refunded in the next fiscal year. District bonded debt shall not issue on terms that could exceed its share of its maximum repayment costs in (b) (iv). Ballot titles for tax or bonded debt increases shall begin, "SHALL (DISTRICT) TAXES BE INCREASED (first, or if phased in, final, full fiscal year dollar increase) ANNUALLY...?" or "SHALL (DISTRICT) DEBT BE INCREASED (principal amount), WITH A REPAYMENT COST OF (maximum total district cost), ...?"

(4) Required elections. Starting November 4, 1992, districts must have voter approval in advance for:

(a) Unless (1) or (6) applies, any new tax, tax rate increase, mill levy above that for the prior year, valuation for assessment ratio increase for a property class, or extension of an expiring tax, or a tax policy change directly causing a net tax revenue gain to any district.

(b) Except for refinancing district bonded debt at a lower interest rate or adding new employees to existing district pension plans, creation of any multiple-fiscal year direct or indirect district debt or other financial obligation whatsoever without adequate present cash reserves pledged irrevocably and held for payments in all future fiscal years.

(5) Emergency reserves. To use for declared emergencies only, each district shall reserve for 1993 1% or more, for 1994 2% or more, and for all later years 3% or more of its fiscal year spending excluding bonded debt service. Unused reserves apply to the next year's reserve.

(6) Emergency taxes. This subsection grants no new taxing power. Emergency property taxes are prohibited. Emergency tax revenue is excluded for purposes of (3) (c) and (7), even if later ratified by voters. Emergency taxes shall also meet all of the following conditions:

(a) A 2/3 majority of the members of each house of the general assembly or of a local district board declares the emergency and imposes the tax by separate recorded roll call votes.

(b) Emergency tax revenue shall be spent only after emergency reserves are depleted, and shall be refunded within 180 days after the emergency ends if not spent on the emergency.

(c) A tax not approved on the next election date 60 days or more after the declaration shall end with that election month.

(7) Spending limits:

(a) The maximum annual percentage change in state fiscal year spending equals inflation plus the percentage change in state population in the prior calendar year, adjusted for revenue changes approved by voters after 1991. Population shall be determined by annual federal census estimates and such number shall be adjusted every decade to match the federal census.
(b) The maximum annual percentage change in each local district's fiscal year spending equals inflation in the prior calendar year plus annual local growth, adjusted for revenue changes approved by voters after 1991 and (8) (b) and (9) reductions.
(c) The maximum annual percentage change in each district's property tax revenue equals inflation in the prior calendar year plus annual local growth, adjusted for property tax revenue changes approved by voters after 1991 and (8) (b) and (9) reductions.
(d) If revenue from sources not excluded from fiscal year spending exceeds these limits in dollars for that fiscal year, the excess shall be refunded in the next fiscal year unless voters approve a revenue change as an offset. Initial district bases are current fiscal year spending and 1991 property tax collected in 1992. Qualification or disqualification as an enterprise shall change district bases and future year limits. Future creation of district bonded debt shall increase, and retiring or refinancing district bonded debt shall lower, fiscal year spending and property tax revenue by the annual debt service so funded. Debt service changes, reductions, (1) and (3) (c) refunds, and voter-approved revenue changes are dollar amounts that are exceptions to, and not part of, any district base. Voter-approved revenue changes do not require a tax rate change.

(8) Revenue limits:

(a) New or increased transfer tax rates on real property are prohibited. No new state real property tax or local district income tax shall be imposed. Neither an income tax rate increase nor a new state definition of taxable income shall apply before the next tax year. Any income tax law change after July 1, 1992 shall also require all taxable net income to be taxed at one rate, excluding refund tax credits or voter-approved tax credits, with no added tax or surcharge.

(b) Each district may enact cumulative uniform exemptions and credits to reduce or end business personal property taxes.

(c) Regardless of reassessment frequency, valuation notices shall be mailed annually and may be appealed annually, with no presumption in favor of any pending valuation. Past or future sales by a lender or government shall also be considered as comparable market sales and their sales prices kept as public records. Actual value shall be stated on all property tax bills and valuation notices and, for residential real property, determined solely by the market approach to appraisal.

(9) State mandates. Except for public education through grade 12 or as required of a local district by federal law, a local district may reduce or end its subsidy to any program delegated to it by the general assembly for administration. For current programs, the state may require 90 days notice and that the adjustment occur in a maximum of three equal annual installments.

Article XI: Public Indebtedness

Section 1. Pledging Credit of State, County, City, Town or School District Forbidden.

Neither the state, nor any county, city, town, township or school district shall lend or pledge the credit or faith thereof, directly or indirectly, in any manner to, or in aid of, any person, company or corporation, public or private, for any amount, or for any purpose whatever; or become responsible for any debt, contract or liability of any person, company or corporation, public or private, in or out of the state.

Section 2. No Aid to Corporations No Joint Ownership By State, County, City, Town, or School District.

Neither the state, nor any county, city, town, township, or school district shall make any donation or grant to, or in aid of, or become a subscriber to, or shareholder in any corporation or company or a joint owner with any person, company, or corporation, public or private, in or out of the state, except as to such ownership as may accrue to the state by escheat, or by forfeiture, by operation or provision of law; and except as to such ownership as may accrue to the state, or to any county, city, town, township, or school district, or to either or any of them, jointly with any person, company, or corporation, by forfeiture or sale of real estate for nonpayment of taxes, or by donation or devise for public use, or by purchase by or on behalf of any or either of them, jointly with any or either of them, under execution in cases of fines, penalties, or forfeiture of recognizance, breach of condition of official bond, or of bond to secure public moneys, or the performance of any contract in which they or any of them may be jointly or severally interested. Nothing in this section shall be construed to prohibit any city or town from becoming a subscriber or shareholder in any corporation or company, public or private, or a joint owner with any person, company, or corporation, public or private, in order to effect the development of energy resources after discovery, or production, transportation, or transmission of energy in whole or in part for the benefit of the inhabitants of such city or town.

Section 2a. Student Loan Program.
The general assembly may by law provide for a student loan program to assist students enrolled in educational institutions.

Section 3. Public Debt of State Limitations.
The state shall not contract any debt by loan in any form, except to provide for casual deficiencies of revenue, erect public buildings for the use of the state, suppress insurrection, defend the state, or, in time of war, assist in defending the United States; and the amount of debt contracted in any one year to provide for deficiencies of revenue shall not exceed one- fourth of a mill on each dollar of valuation of taxable property within the state, and the aggregate amount of such debt shall not at any time exceed three- fourths of a mill on each dollar of said valuation, until the valuation shall equal one hundred millions of dollars, and thereafter such debt shall not exceed one hundred thousand dollars; and the debt incurred in any one year for erection of public buildings shall not exceed one- half mill on each dollar of said valuation; and the aggregate amount of such debt shall never at any time exceed the sum of fifty thousand dollars (except as provided in section 5 of this article), and in all cases the valuation in this section mentioned shall be that of the assessment last preceding the creation of said debt.

Section 4. Law Creating Debt.
In no case shall any debt above mentioned in this article be created except by a law which shall be irrepealable, until the indebtedness therein provided for shall have been fully paid or discharged; such law shall specify the purposes to which the funds so raised shall be applied, and provide for the levy of a tax sufficient to pay the interest on and extinguish the principal of such debt within the time limited by such law for the payment thereof, which in the case of debts contracted for the erection of public buildings and supplying deficiencies of revenue shall not be less than ten nor more than fifteen years, and the funds arising from the collection of any such tax shall not be applied to any other purpose than that provided in the law levying the same, and when the debt thereby created shall be paid or

discharged, such tax shall cease and the balance, if any, to the credit of the fund shall immediately be placed to the credit of the general fund of the state.

Section 5. Debt for Public Buildings How Created.

A debt for the purpose of erecting public buildings may be created by law as provided for in section four of this article, not exceeding in the aggregate three mills on each dollar of said valuation; provided, that before going into effect, such law shall be ratified by the vote of a majority of such qualified electors of the state as shall vote thereon at a general election under such regulations as the general assembly may prescribe.

Section 6. Local Government Debt.

(1) No political subdivision of the state shall contract any general obligation debt by loan in any form, whether individually or by contract pursuant to article XIV, section 18 (2) (a) of this constitution except by adoption of a legislative measure which shall be irrepealable until the indebtedness therein provided for shall have been fully paid or discharged, specifying the purposes to which the funds to be raised shall be applied and providing for the levy of a tax which together with such other revenue, assets, or funds as may be pledged shall be sufficient to pay the interest and principal of such debt. Except as may be otherwise provided by the charter of a home rule city and county, city, or town for debt incurred by such city and county, city, or town, no such debt shall be created unless the question of incurring the same be submitted to and approved by a majority of the qualified taxpaying electors voting thereon, as the term "qualified taxpaying elector" shall be defined by statute.
(2) Except as may be otherwise provided by the charter of a home rule city and county, city, or town, the general assembly shall establish by statute limitations on the authority of any political subdivision to incur general obligation indebtedness in any form whether individually or by contract pursuant to article XIV, section 18 (2) (a) of this constitution.
(3) Debts contracted by a home rule city and county, city, or

town, statutory city or town or service authority for the purposes of supplying water shall be excepted from the operation of this section.

Section 7 State and Political Subdivisions May Give Assistance to Any Political Subdivision.

No provision of this constitution shall be construed to prevent the state or any political subdivision from giving direct or indirect financial support to any political subdivision as may be authorized by general statute.

Section 8. City Indebtedness; Ordinance, Tax, Water Obligations Excepted.

Repealed.

Section 9. This Article Not to Affect Prior Obligations.

Repealed.

Section 10. 1976 Winter Olympics.

Deleted by amendment.

Article XII: Officers

Section 1. When Office Expires Suspension by Law.
Every person holding any civil office under the state or any municipality therein, shall, unless removed according to law, exercise the duties of such office until his successor is duly qualified; but this shall not apply to members of the general assembly, nor to members of any board or assembly, two or more of whom are elected at the same time. The general assembly may, by law, provide for suspending any officer in his functions pending impeachment or prosecution for misconduct in office.

Section 2. Personal Attention Required.
No person shall hold any office or employment of trust or profit, under the laws of the state or any ordinance of any municipality therein, without devoting his personal attention to the duties of the same.

Section 3. Defaulting Collector Disqualified from Office.
No person who is now or hereafter may become a collector or receiver of public money, or the deputy or assistant of such collector or receiver, and who shall have become a defaulter in his office, shall be eligible to or assume the duties of any office of trust or profit in this state, under the laws thereof, or of any municipality therein, until he shall have accounted for and paid over all public money for which he may be accountable.

Section 4. Disqualifications from Holding Office of Trust or Profit.
No person hereafter convicted of embezzlement of public moneys, bribery, perjury, solicitation of bribery, or subornation of perjury, shall be eligible to the general assembly, or capable of holding any office of trust or profit in this state.

Section 5. Investigation of State and County Treasurers.
The district court of each county shall, at each term thereof, specially give in charge to the grand jury, if there be one, the laws regulating the accountability of the county treasurer, and shall appoint a committee of such grand jury, or of other reputable persons not exceeding five, to investigate the official accounts and affairs of the treasurer of such county, and report to the court the condition thereof. The judge of the district court may appoint a like committee in vacation at any time, but not oftener than once in every three months. The district court of the county wherein the seat of government may be shall have the like power to appoint committees to investigate the official accounts and affairs of the state treasurer and the auditor of state.

Section 6. Bribery of Officers Defined.
Any civil officer or member of the general assembly who shall solicit, demand or receive, or consent to receive, directly or indirectly, for himself or for another, from any company, corporation or person, any money, office, appointment, employment, testimonial, reward, thing of value or enjoyment or of personal advantage or promise thereof, for his vote, official influence or action, or for withholding the same, or with an understanding that his official influence or action shall be in any way influenced thereby, or who shall solicit or demand any such money or advantage, matter or thing aforesaid for another, as the consideration of his vote, official influence or action, or for withholding the same, or shall give or withhold his vote, official influence or action, in consideration of the payment or promise of such money, advantage, matter or thing to another, shall be held guilty of bribery, or solicitation of bribery, as the case may be, within the meaning of this constitution, and shall incur the disabilities provided thereby for such offense, and such additional punishment as is or shall be prescribed by law.

Section 7. Bribery Corrupt Solicitation.

(1) Any person who directly or indirectly offers, gives, or promises any money or thing of value or privilege to any member of the general assembly or to any other public officer in the executive or judicial department of the state government to influence him in the performance of any of his public or official powers or duties is guilty of bribery and subject to such punishment therefore as may be prescribed by law.
(2) The offense of corrupt solicitation of members of the general assembly or of public officers of the state or of any political subdivision thereof and any occupation or practice of solicitation of such members or officers to influence their official action shall be defined by law and shall be punished by fine, imprisonment, or both.

Section 8. Oath of Civil Officers.
Every civil officer, except members of the general assembly and such inferior officers as may be by law exempted, shall, before he enters upon the duties of his office, take and subscribe an oath or affirmation to support the constitution of the United States and of the state of Colorado, and to faithfully perform the duties of the office upon which he shall be about to enter.

Section 9. Oaths Where Filed.
Officers of the executive department and judges of the supreme and district courts, and district attorneys, shall file their oaths of office with the secretary of state; every other officer shall file his oath of office with the county clerk of the county wherein he shall have been elected.

Section 10. Refusal to Qualify Vacancy.
If any person elected or appointed to any office shall refuse or neglect to qualify therein within the time prescribed by law, such office shall be deemed vacant.

Section 11. Elected Public Officers Term Salary Vacancy.

Elected public officers - term - salary - vacancy. No law shall extend the term of any elected public officer after his election or appointment nor shall the salary of any elected public officer be increased or decreased during the term of office for which he was elected. The term of office of any officer elected to fill a vacancy shall terminate at the expiration of the term during which the vacancy occurred.

Section 12. Duel Disqualifies for Office.

Deleted by amendment.

Section 13. Personnel System of State Merit System.

(1) Appointments and promotions to offices and employments in the state personnel system shall be made according to merit and fitness, to be ascertained by a comparative analysis of candidates based on objective criteria without regard to race, creed, color, or political affiliation. A numerical or nonnumerical method may be used for the comparative analysis of candidates.

(2)(a) The state personnel system shall comprise all appointive public officers and employees of the state, except the following:

(I) Members of the public utilities commission, the industrial commission of Colorado, the state board of land commissioners, the Colorado tax commission, the state parole board, and the state personnel board;

(II) Members of any board or commission serving without compensation except for per diem allowances provided by law and reimbursement of expenses;

(III) The employees in the offices of the governor and the lieutenant governor whose functions are confined to such offices and whose duties are concerned only with the administration thereof;

(IV) Appointees to fill vacancies in elective offices;

(V) One deputy of each elective officer other than the governor and lieutenant governor specified in section 1 of article IV of this constitution;

(VI) Officers otherwise specified in this constitution;

(VII) Faculty members of educational institutions and departments not reformatory or charitable in character, and such administrators thereof as may be exempt by law;

(VIII) Students and inmates in state educational or other institutions employed therein;

(IX) Attorneys at law serving as assistant attorneys general;

(X) Members, officers, and employees of the legislative and judicial departments of the state, unless otherwise specifically provided in this constitution;

(XI) Subject to the approval of the state personnel director, the following persons from each principal department: Deputy department heads, chief financial officers, public information officers, legislative liaisons, human resource directors, and executive assistants to the department heads; and

(XII) Subject to the approval of the state personnel director, senior executive service employees.

(b) The total number of employees exempted from the state personnel system pursuant to subparagraphs (XI) and (XII) of paragraph (a) of this subsection (2) shall not exceed an amount equal to one percent of the total number of persons in the state personnel system.

(3) Officers and employees within the judicial department, other than judges and justices, may be included within the personnel system of the state upon determination by the supreme court, sitting en banc, that such would be in the best interests of the state.

(4) Where authorized by law, any political subdivision of this state may contract with the state personnel board for personnel services.

(5) The person to be appointed to any position under the state personnel system shall be one of the six persons ranking highest on the eligible list for such position, or such lesser number as qualify, as determined from the comparative analysis process, subject to limitations set forth in rules of the state personnel board applicable to multiple appointments from any such list.

(6)(a) Except as set forth in paragraph (b) of this subsection (6), all appointees shall reside in the state, but applications need not be limited to residents of the state as to those positions the state personnel board or the state personnel director determines cannot be readily filled from among residents of this state.
(b) If a position is for work that is to be performed primarily at a location that is within thirty miles of the state border:

(I) Applications for the position are not limited to residents of the state; and
(II) An appointee to the position is not required to be a resident of the state.

(7) The head of each principal department shall be the appointing authority for the employees of his office and for heads of divisions, within the personnel system, ranking next below the head of such department. Heads of such divisions shall be the appointing authorities for all positions in the personnel system within their respective divisions. Nothing in this subsection shall be construed to affect the supreme executive powers of the governor prescribed in section 2 of article IV of this constitution.
(8) Persons in the personnel system of the state shall hold their respective positions during efficient service or until reaching retirement age, as provided by law. They shall be graded and compensated according to standards of efficient service which shall be the same for all persons having like duties. A person certified to any class or position in the personnel system may be dismissed, suspended, or otherwise disciplined by the appointing authority upon written findings of failure to comply with standards of efficient service or competence, or for willful misconduct, willful failure or inability to perform his duties, or final conviction of a felony or any other offense which involves moral turpitude, or written charges thereof may be filed by any person with the appointing authority, which shall be promptly determined. Any action of the appointing authority taken under this subsection shall be subject to appeal to the state personnel

board, with the right to be heard thereby in person or by counsel, or both.

(9)(a) The state personnel director may authorize the temporary employment of persons, not to exceed nine months, during which time an eligible list shall be provided for permanent positions. No other temporary or emergency employment shall be permitted under the state personnel system.
(b) Nothing in paragraph (a) of this subsection (9) shall be construed as permitting the appointment of a temporary employee for the purpose of eliminating a permanent position from the state personnel system.

(10) The state personnel board shall establish probationary periods for all persons initially appointed, but not to exceed twelve months for any class or position. After satisfactory completion of any such period, the person shall be certified to such class or position within the personnel system, but unsatisfactory performance shall be grounds for dismissal by the appointing authority during such period without right of appeal.
(11) Persons certified to classes and positions under the classified civil service of the state immediately prior to July 1, 1971, persons having served for six months or more as provisional or acting provisional employees in such positions immediately prior to such date, and all persons having served six months or more in positions not within the classified civil service immediately prior to such date but included in the personnel system by this section, shall be certified to comparable positions, and grades and classifications, under the personnel system, and shall not be subject to probationary periods of employment. All other persons in positions under the personnel system shall be subject to the provisions of this section concerning initial appointment on or after such date.

Section 14. State Personnel Board State Personnel Director.

(1) There is hereby created a state personnel board to consist of five members, three of whom shall be appointed by the governor with the consent of the senate, and two of whom shall be elected by persons certified to classes and positions in the state personnel system in the manner prescribed by law. Each member appointed or elected prior to January 1, 2013, shall serve for a term of five years. Each member appointed or elected on or after January 1, 2013, shall serve for a term of three years. No member shall serve more than two terms of office, regardless of whether a term is a full term or a partial term filling a vacancy. Each member of the board shall be a qualified elector of the state, but shall not be otherwise an officer or employee of the state or of any state employee organization, and shall receive such compensation as shall be fixed by law.

(2)(a) Two of the appointed members of the state personnel board serve at the pleasure of the governor. Both elected members of the board and the appointed member specified in paragraph (b) of this subsection (2) may be removed by the governor for willful misconduct in office, willful failure or inability to perform his or her duties, final conviction of a felony or of any other offense involving moral turpitude, or by reason of permanent disability interfering with the performance of his or her duties, which removal shall be subject to judicial review. Any vacancy in office shall be filled in the same manner as the selection of the person vacating the office, and for the unexpired term.

(b) The member of the board who is appointed for a term commencing on July 1, 2013, and the successors to that position do not serve at the pleasure of the governor.

(3) The state personnel board shall adopt, and may from time to time amend or repeal, rules to implement the provisions of this section and sections 13 and 15 of this article, as amended, and laws enacted pursuant thereto, including but not limited to rules concerning standardization of positions, determination of grades of positions, standards of efficient and competent service, grievance procedures, appeals from actions by appointing authorities, and conduct of hearings by hearing officers where authorized by law.

(4) There is hereby created the department of personnel, which shall be one of the principal departments of the executive department, the head of which shall be the state personnel director, who shall be appointed under qualifications established by law. The state personnel director shall be responsible for the administration of the personnel system of the state under this constitution and laws enacted pursuant thereto and the rules adopted thereunder by the state personnel board.

(5) Adequate appropriations shall be made to carry out the purposes of this section and section 13 of this article.

Section 15. Veterans' Preference.

(1)(a)(I) The minimum requirements for a candidate to be placed on an eligible list for a position shall be the same for each candidate for appointment or employment in the state personnel system or in any comparable civil service or merit system of any agency or political subdivision of the state, including any municipality chartered or to be chartered under article XX of this constitution.

(II) If a numerical method is used for the comparative analysis based on objective criteria, applicants entitled to preference under this section shall be given preference in accordance with paragraphs (b) to (e) of this subsection (1). If a nonnumerical method is used, applicants entitled to preference under this section shall be added to the interview eligible list.

(b) Five points shall be added to the comparative analysis score of each candidate who is separated under honorable conditions and who, other than for training purposes, (i) served in any branch of the armed forces of the United States during any period of any declared war or any undeclared war or other armed hostilities against an armed foreign enemy, or (ii) served on active duty in any such branch in any campaign or expedition for which a campaign badge is authorized.

(c) Ten points shall be added to the comparative analysis score of any candidate who has so served, other than for training purposes, and who, because of disability incurred in the line of duty, is receiving monetary compensation or disability retired benefits by reason of public laws administered by the department of defense or the veterans administration, or any successor thereto.

(d) Five points shall be added to the comparative analysis score of any candidate who is the surviving spouse of any person who was or would have been entitled to additional points under paragraph (b) or (c) of this subsection (1) or of any person who died during such service or as a result of service-connected cause while on active duty in any such branch, other than for training purposes.

(e) No more than a total of ten points shall be added to the comparative analysis score of any such candidate pursuant to this subsection (1).

(2) The certificate of the department of defense or of the veterans administration, or any successor thereto, shall be conclusive proof of service under honorable conditions or of disability or death incurred in the line of duty during such service.

(3)(a) When a reduction in the work force of the state or any such political subdivision thereof becomes necessary because of lack of work or curtailment of funds, employees not eligible for preference under subsection (1) of this section shall be separated before those so entitled who have the same or more service in the employment of the state or such political subdivision, counting both military service for which such preference is given and such employment with the state or such political subdivision, as the case may be, from which the employee is to be separated.

(b) In the case of such a person eligible for preference who has completed twenty or more years of active military service, no military service shall be counted in determining length of service in respect to such retention rights. In the case of such a person who has completed less than twenty years of such military service, no more than ten years of service under subsection (1)(b) (i) and (ii) shall be counted in determining such length of service for such retention rights.

(4) The state personnel board and each comparable supervisory or administrative board of any such civil service or merit system of any agency of the state or any such political subdivision thereof shall implement the provisions of this section to assure that all persons entitled to preference in a comparative analysis and retention shall enjoy their full privileges and rights granted by this section.

(5) No person shall receive preference pursuant to this section with respect to a promotional opportunity. Any promotional opportunity that is also open to persons other than employees for whom such appointment would be a promotion, shall be considered a promotional opportunity for the purposes of this section.

(6) Repealed.

(7) This section shall be in full force and effect on and after July 1, 1971, and shall grant veterans' preference to all persons who have served in the armed forces of the United States in any declared or undeclared war, conflict, engagement, expedition, or campaign for which a campaign badge has been authorized, and who meet the requirements of service or disability, or both, as provided in this section. This section shall apply to all public employment opportunities, except as set forth in subsection (5) of this section, conducted on or after such date, and it shall be in all respects self-executing.

Article XIII: Impeachments

Section 1. House Impeach Senate Try Conviction When Chief Justice Presides.

The house of representatives shall have the sole power of impeachment. The concurrence of a majority of all the members shall be necessary to an impeachment. All impeachments shall be tried by the senate, and when sitting for that purpose, the senators shall be upon oath or affirmation to do justice according to law and evidence. When the governor or lieutenant -governor is on trial, the chief justice of the supreme court shall preside. No person shall be convicted without a concurrence of two -thirds of the senators elected.

Section 2. Who Liable to Impeachment Judgment No Bar to Prosecution.

The governor and other state and judicial officers, shall be liable to impeachment for high crimes or misdemeanors or malfeasance in office, but judgment in such cases shall only extend to removal from office and disqualification to hold any office of honor, trust or profit in the state. The party, whether convicted or acquitted, shall, nevertheless, be liable to prosecution, trial, judgment and punishment according to law.
Officers Not Subject to Impeachment Subject to Removal.
All officers not liable to impeachment shall be subject to removal for misconduct or malfeasance in office in such manner as may be provided by law.

Section 3. Officers Not Subject to Impeachment Subject to Removal.

All officers not liable to impeachment shall be subject to removal for misconduct or malfeasance in office in such manner as may be provided by law.

Article XIV: Counties

Section 1. Counties of State.
The several counties of the territory of Colorado as they now exist, are hereby declared to be counties of the state.

Section 2. Removal of County Seats.
The general assembly shall have no power to remove the county seat of any county, but the removal of county seats shall be provided for by general law, and no county seat shall be removed unless a majority of the registered electors of the county, voting on the proposition at a general election vote therefore; and no such proposition shall be submitted oftener than once in four years, and no person shall vote on such proposition who shall not have resided in the county six months and in the election precinct ninety days next preceding such election.

Section 3. Striking Off Territory Vote.
Except as otherwise provided by statute, no part of the territory of any county shall be stricken off and added to an adjoining county, without first submitting the question to the registered electors of the county from which the territory is proposed to be stricken off; nor unless a majority of all the registered electors of said county voting on the question shall vote therefore.

Section 4. New County Shall Pay Proportion of Debt.
In all cases of the establishment of any new county, the new county shall be held to pay its ratable proportion of all then existing liabilities, of the county or counties from which such new county shall be formed.

Section 5. Part Stricken Off Pay Proportion of Debt.
When any part of a county is stricken off and attached to another county, the part stricken off shall be held to pay its ratable proportion of all then existing liabilities of the county from which it is taken.

Section 6. County Commissioners Election Term.

In each county having a population of less than seventy thousand there shall be elected, for a term of four years each, three county commissioners who shall hold sessions for the transaction of county business as provided by law; any two of whom shall constitute a quorum for the transaction of business. Two of said commissioners shall be elected at the general election in the year nineteen hundred and four, and at the general election every four years thereafter; and the other one of said commissioners shall be elected at the general election in the year nineteen hundred and six, and at the general election every four years thereafter; provided, that when the population of any county shall equal or exceed seventy thousand, the board of county commissioners may consist of five members, any three of whom shall constitute a quorum for the transaction of business. Three of said commissioners in said county shall be elected at the general election in the year nineteen hundred and four, and at the general election every four years thereafter; and the other two of said commissioners in such county shall be elected at the general election in the year nineteen hundred and six and every four years thereafter; and all of such commissioners shall be elected for the term of four years.

The term of office of the county commissioners in each county that expires in January, 1904, is hereby extended to the second Tuesday in January, A.D. 1905, and the term of office of the county commissioners that expires in January, 1906, is hereby extended to the second Tuesday in January, A.D. 1907; and in counties having a population of more than seventy thousand, the term of office of the commissioners that expires in 1904 shall be extended to the second Tuesday in January, 1905, and the term of office of the county commissioners that expires in 1906 is hereby extended to the second Tuesday in January, 1907. This section shall govern, except as hereafter otherwise expressly directed or permitted by constitutional enactment.

Section 7. Officers Compensation.

Repealed.

Section 8. County Officers Election Term Salary.

There shall be elected in each county, at the same time at which members of the general assembly are elected, commencing in the year nineteen hundred and fifty-four, and every four years thereafter, one county clerk, who shall be ex officio recorder of deeds and clerk of the board of county commissioners; one sheriff; one coroner; one treasurer who shall be collector of taxes; one county superintendent of schools; one county surveyor; one county assessor; and one county attorney who may be elected or appointed, as shall be provided by law; and such officers shall be paid such salary or compensation, either from the fees, perquisites and emoluments of their respective offices, or from the general county fund, as may be provided by law. The term of office of all such officials shall be four years, and they shall take office on the second Tuesday in January next following their election, or at such other time as may be provided by law. The officers herein named elected at the general election in 1954 shall hold their respective offices until the second Tuesday of January, 1959.

Section 9. Vacancies How Filled.

In case of a vacancy occurring in the office of county commissioner a vacancy committee of the same political party as the vacating commissioner constituted as provided by law shall, by a majority vote, fill the vacancy by appointment within ten days after occurrence of the vacancy. If the vacancy committee fails to fill the vacancy within ten days after occurrence of the vacancy, the governor shall fill the same by appointment within fifteen days after occurrence of the vacancy. The person appointed to fill a vacancy in the office of county commissioner shall be a member of the same political party, if any, as the vacating commissioner. In case of a vacancy in any other county office, or in any precinct office, the board of county commissioners shall fill the same by appointment. Any person appointed pursuant to this section shall hold the office until the next general election, or until the vacancy is filled by election according to law.

Section 10. Elector Only Eligible to County Office.
No person shall be eligible to any county office unless he shall be a qualified elector; nor unless he shall have resided in the county one year preceding his election.

Section 11. Justices of the Peace Constables.

Repealed.

Section 12. Other Officers.
The general assembly shall provide for the election or appointment of such other county officers and such municipal officers of statutory cities and towns as public convenience may require; and their terms of office shall be as prescribed by statute.

Section 13. Classification of Cities and Towns.
The general assembly shall provide, by general laws, for the organization and classification of cities and towns. The number of such classes shall not exceed four; and the powers of each class shall be defined by general laws, so that all municipal corporations of the same class shall possess the same powers and be subject to the same restrictions.

Section 14. Existing Cities and Towns May Come under General Law.
The general assembly shall also make provision, by general law, whereby any city, town or village, incorporated by any special or local law, may elect to become subject to and be governed by the general law relating to such corporations.

Section 15. Compensation and Fees of County Officers.
The general assembly shall fix the compensation of county officers in this state by law, and shall establish scales of fees to be charged and collected by such county officers. All such fees shall be paid into the county general fund.
When fixing the compensation of county officers, the general assembly shall give due consideration to county variations,

including population; the number of persons residing in unincorporated areas; assessed valuation; motor vehicle registrations; building permits; military installations; and such other factors as may be necessary to prepare compensation schedules that reflect variations in the workloads and responsibilities of county officers and in the tax resources of the several counties.

The compensation of any county officer shall be increased or decreased only when the compensation of all county officers within the same county, or when the compensation for the same county officer within the several counties of the state, is increased or decreased.

Except for the schedule of increased compensation for county officers enacted by the general assembly to become effective on January 1, 1969, county officers shall not thereafter have their compensation increased or decreased during the terms of office to which they have been elected or appointed.

Section 16. County Home Rule.

(1) Notwithstanding the provisions of sections 6, 8, 9, 10, 12, and 15 of this article, the registered electors of each county of the state are hereby vested with the power to adopt a home rule charter establishing the organization and structure of county government consistent with this article and statutes enacted pursuant hereto.

(2) The general assembly shall provide by statute procedures under which the registered electors of any county may adopt, amend, and repeal a county home rule charter. Action to initiate home rule may be by petition, signed by not less than five percent of the registered electors of the county in which home rule is sought, or by any other procedure authorized by statute. No county home rule charter, amendment thereto, or repeal thereof, shall become effective until approved by a majority of the registered electors of such county voting thereon.

(3) A home rule county shall provide all mandatory county functions, services, and facilities and shall exercise all mandatory powers as may be required by statute.

(4) A home rule county shall be empowered to provide such permissive functions, services, and facilities and to exercise such permissive powers as may be authorized by statute applicable to all home rule counties, except as may be otherwise prohibited or limited by charter or this constitution.

(5) The provisions of sections 6, 8, 9, 10, 12, and 15 of article XIV of this constitution shall apply to counties adopting a home rule charter only to such extent as may be provided in said charter.

Section 17. Service Authorities.

(1) (a) The general assembly shall provide by statute for the organization, structure, functions, services, facilities, and powers of service authorities pursuant to the following requirements:

(b) A service authority may be formed only upon the approval of a majority of the registered electors voting thereon in the territory to be included.

(c) The territory within a service authority may include all or part of one county or home rule county or all or part of two or more adjoining counties or home rule counties, but shall not include only a part of any city and county, home rule city or town, or statutory city or town at the time of formation of the service authority. No more than one service authority shall be established in any territory and, in no event, shall a service authority be formed in the metropolitan area composed of the city and county of Denver, and Adams, Arapahoe, and Jefferson counties which does not include all of the city and county of Denver and all or portions of Adams, Arapahoe, and Jefferson counties.

(d) The boundaries of any service authority shall not be such as to create any enclave.

(e) No territory shall be included within the boundaries of more than one service authority.

(2) (a) The general assembly shall also provide by statute for:
(b) The inclusion and exclusion of territory in or from a service authority;
(c) The dissolution of a service authority;
(d) The merger of all or a part of two or more adjacent service authorities, except that such merger shall require the approval of a majority of the registered electors voting thereon in each of the affected service authorities; and,
(e) The boundaries of any service authority or any special taxing districts therein or the method by which such boundaries are to be determined or changed; and
(f) The method for payment of any election expenses.

(3)(a) The general assembly shall designate by statute the functions, services, and facilities which may be provided by a service authority, and the manner in which the members of the governing body of any service authority shall be elected from compact districts of approximately equal population by the registered electors of the authority, including the terms and qualifications of such members. The general assembly may provide that members of the governing body may be elected by a vote of each compact district or by an at-large vote or combination thereof. Notwithstanding any provision in this constitution or the charter of any home rule city and county, city, town, or county to the contrary, mayors, councilmen, trustees, and county commissioners may additionally hold elective office with a service authority and serve therein either with or without compensation, as provided by statute.
(b) A service authority shall provide any function, service, or facility designated by statute and authorized as provided in paragraphs (c) and (d) of this subsection.
(c) All propositions to provide functions, services, or facilities shall be submitted, either individually or jointly, to the registered electors in the manner and form prescribed by law.
(d) Each such function, service, or facility shall be authorized if approved by a majority of the registered electors of the authority voting thereon; but if the service authority includes territory in more than one county, approval shall also require a majority of

the registered electors of the authority voting thereon in those included portions of each of the affected counties.

(e) Notwithstanding the provisions of paragraphs (b), (c), and (d) of this subsection, where, upon formation of a service authority, any function, service, or facility is already being provided in at least four counties or portions thereof by a single special district, regional planning commission or metropolitan council, or an association of political subdivisions, the general assembly may provide, without a vote of the registered electors, for assumption by one or more service authorities of such function, service, or facility.

(f) Notwithstanding the provisions of paragraphs (b), (c), and (d) of this subsection, a service authority may contract with any other political subdivision to provide or receive any function, service, or facility designated by statute; but a service authority shall not be invested with any taxing power as a consequence of such contract.

(4) (a) A service authority shall be a body corporate and a political subdivision of the state.

(b) Any other provision of this constitution to the contrary notwithstanding, any service authority formed under this article and the statutes pursuant thereto may exercise such powers to accomplish the purposes and to provide the authorized functions, services, and facilities of such authority as the general assembly may provide by statute.

(c) Notwithstanding the provisions of article XX of this constitution, any authorized function, service, or facility may be provided exclusively by the authority or concurrently with other jurisdictions as may be prescribed by statute, subject to the provisions of subsections (3) (c), (3) (d), (3) (e), and (3) (f) of this section.

Section 18. Intergovernmental Relationships.

(1) (a) Any other provisions of this constitution to the contrary notwithstanding:

(b) The general assembly may provide by statute for the terms and conditions under which one or more service authorities may succeed to the rights, properties, and other assets and assume the obligations of any other political subdivision included partially or entirely within such authority, incident to the powers vested in, and the functions, services, and facilities authorized to be provided by the service authority, whether vested and authorized at the time of the formation of the service authority or subsequent thereto; and,

(c) The general assembly may provide by statute for the terms and conditions under which a county, home rule county, city and county, home rule city or town, statutory city or town, or quasi-municipal corporation, or any combination thereof may succeed to the rights, properties, and other assets and assume the obligations of any quasi-municipal corporation located partially or entirely within its boundaries.

(d) The general assembly may provide by statute procedures whereby any county, home rule county, city and county, home rule city or town, statutory city or town, or service authority may establish special taxing districts.

(2) (a) Nothing in this constitution shall be construed to prohibit the state or any of its political subdivisions from cooperating or contracting with one another or with the government of the United States to provide any function, service, or facility lawfully authorized to each of the cooperating or contracting units, including the sharing of costs, the imposition of taxes, or the incurring of debt.

(b) Nothing in this constitution shall be construed to prohibit the authorization by statute of a separate governmental entity as an instrument to be used through voluntary participation by cooperating or contracting political subdivisions.

(c) Nothing in this constitution shall be construed to prohibit any political subdivision of the state from contracting with private persons, associations, or corporations for the provision of any legally authorized functions, services, or facilities within or without its boundaries.

(d) Nothing in this constitution shall be construed to prohibit the general assembly from providing by statute for state imposed and collected taxes to be shared with and distributed to political subdivisions of the state except that this provision shall not in any way limit the powers of home rule cities and towns.

Article XV: Corporations

Section 1. Unused Charters or Grants of Privilege.

Repealed.

Section 2. Corporate Charters Created by General Law.
No charter of incorporation shall be granted, extended, changed or amended by special law, except for such municipal, charitable, educational, penal or reformatory corporations as are or may be under the control of the state; but the general assembly shall provide by general laws for the organization of corporations hereafter to be created.

Section 3. Power to Revoke, Alter or Annul Charter.
The general assembly shall have the power to alter, revoke or annul any charter of incorporation now existing and revocable at the adoption of this constitution, or any that may hereafter be created, whenever in their opinion it may be injurious to the citizens of the state, in such manner, however, that no injustice shall be done to the corporators.

Section 4. Railroads Common Carriers Construction Intersection.
All railroads shall be public highways, and all railroad companies shall be common carriers. Any association or corporation organized for the purpose, shall have the right to construct and operate a railroad between any designated points within this state, and to connect at the state line with railroads of other states and territories. Every railroad company shall have the right with its road to intersect, connect with or cross any other railroad.

Section 5. Consolidation of Parallel Lines Forbidden.
No railroad corporation, or the lessees or managers thereof, shall consolidate its stock, property or franchises with any other railroad corporation owning or having under its control a parallel or competing line.

Section 6. Equal Rights of Public to Transportation.

All individuals, associations and corporations shall have equal rights to have persons and property transported over any railroad in this state, and no undue or unreasonable discrimination shall be made in charges or in facilities for transportation of freight or passengers within the state, and no railroad company, nor any lessee, manager or employee thereof, shall give any preference to individuals, associations or corporations in furnishing cars or motive power.

Section 7. Existing Railroads to File Acceptance of Continuation.

Repealed.

Section 8. Eminent Domain Police Power Not to Be Abridged.

The right of eminent domain shall never be abridged nor so construed as to prevent the general assembly from taking the property and franchises of incorporated companies, and subjecting them to public use, the same as the property of individuals; and the police power of the state shall never be abridged or so construed as to permit corporations to conduct their business in such manner as to infringe the equal rights of individuals or the general well- being of the state.

Section 9. Fictitious Stock, Bonds Increase of Stock.

No corporation shall issue stocks or bonds, except for labor done, service performed, or money or property actually received, and all fictitious increase of stock or indebtedness shall be void. The stock of corporations shall not be increased except in pursuance of general law, nor without the consent of the persons holding a majority of the stock, first obtained at a meeting held after at least thirty days' notice given in pursuance of law.

Section 10. Foreign Corporations Place Agent.
No foreign corporation shall do any business in this state without having one or more known places of business, and an authorized agent or agents in the same, upon whom process may be served.

Section 11. Street Railroads Consent of Municipality.
No street railroad shall be constructed within any city, town, or incorporated village, without the consent of the local authorities having the control of the street or highway proposed to be occupied by such street railroad.

Section 12. Retrospective Laws Not to Be Passed.
The general assembly shall pass no law for the benefit of a railroad or other corporation, or any individual or association of individuals, retrospective in its operation, or which imposes on the people of any county or municipal subdivision of the state, a new liability in respect to transactions or considerations already past.

Section 13. Telegraph Lines Consolidation.
Any association or corporation, or the lessees or managers thereof, organized for the purpose, or any individual, shall have the right to construct and maintain lines of telegraph within this state, and to connect the same with other lines, and the general assembly shall, by general law, of uniform operation, provide reasonable regulations to give full effect to this section. No telegraph company shall consolidate with, or hold a controlling interest in, the stock or bonds of any other telegraph company owning or having the control of a competing line, or acquire, by purchase or otherwise, any other competing line of telegraph.

Section 14. Railroad or Telegraph Companies Consolidating with Foreign Companies.
If any railroad, telegraph, express or other corporation organized under any of the laws of this state, shall consolidate, by sale or otherwise, with any railroad, telegraph, express or other corporation organized under any laws of any other state or

territory or of the United States, the same shall not thereby become a foreign corporation, but the courts of this state shall retain jurisdiction over that part of the corporate property within the limits of the state in all matters which may arise, as if said consolidation had not taken place.

Section 15. Contracts with Employees Releasing from Liability Void.

It shall be unlawful for any person, company or corporation to require of its servants or employees, as a condition of their employment or otherwise, any contract or agreement, whereby such person, company or corporation shall be released or discharged from liability or responsibility on account of personal injuries received by such servants or employees while in the service of such person, company or corporation, by reason of the negligence of such person, company or corporation, or the agents or employees thereof, and such contracts shall be absolutely null and void.

Article XVI: Mining and Irrigation

Mines

Section 1. Commissioner of Mines.
There shall be established and maintained the office of commissioner of mines, the duties and salaries of which shall be prescribed by law. When said office shall be established, the governor shall, with the advice and consent of the senate, appoint thereto a person known to be competent, whose term of office shall be four years.

Section 2. Ventilation Employment of Children.
The general assembly shall provide by law for the proper ventilation of mines, the construction of escapement shafts, and such other appliances as may be necessary to protect the health and secure the safety of the workmen therein; and shall prohibit the employment in the mines of children under twelve years of age.

Section 3. Drainage.
The general assembly may make such regulations from time to time, as may be necessary for the proper and equitable drainage of mines.

Section 4. Mining, Metallurgy, in Public Institutions.
The general assembly may provide that the science of mining and metallurgy be taught in one or more of the institutions of learning under the patronage of the state.

Irrigation

Section 5. Water of Streams Public Property.
The water of every natural stream, not heretofore appropriated, within the state of Colorado, is hereby declared to be the property of the public, and the same is dedicated to the use of the people of the state, subject to appropriation as hereinafter provided.

Section 6. **Diverting Unappropriated Water Priority Preferred Uses.**

The right to divert the unappropriated waters of any natural stream to beneficial uses shall never be denied. Priority of appropriation shall give the better right as between those using the water for the same purpose; but when the waters of any natural stream are not sufficient for the service of all those desiring the use of the same, those using the water for domestic purposes shall have the preference over those claiming for any other purpose, and those using the water for agricultural purposes shall have preference over those using the same for manufacturing purposes.

Section 7. **Right of way for Ditches, Flumes.**

All persons and corporations shall have the right-of-way across public, private and corporate lands for the construction of ditches, canals and flumes for the purpose of conveying water for domestic purposes, for the irrigation of agricultural lands, and for mining and manufacturing purposes, and for drainage, upon payment of just compensation.

Section 8. **County Commissioners to Fix Rates for Water, When.**

The general assembly shall provide by law that the board of county commissioners in their respective counties, shall have power, when application is made to them by either party interested, to establish reasonable maximum rates to be charged for the use of water, whether furnished by individuals or corporations.

Article XVII: Militia

Section 1. Persons Subject to Service
The militia of the state shall consist of all able-bodied male residents of the state between the ages of eighteen and forty-five years; except, such persons as may be exempted by the laws of the United States, or of the state.

Section 2. Organization Equipment Discipline
The organization, equipment and discipline of the militia shall conform as nearly as practicable, to the regulations for the government of the armies of the United States.

Section 3. Officers How Chosen
The governor shall appoint all general, field and staff officers and commission them. Each company shall elect its own officers, who shall be commissioned by the governor; but if any company shall fail to elect such officers within the time prescribed by law, they may be appointed by the governor.

Section 4. Armories
The general assembly shall provide for the safekeeping of the public arms, military records, relics and banners of the state.

Section 5. Exemption in Time of Peace
No person having conscientious scruples against bearing arms shall be compelled to do militia duty in time of peace.

Article XVIII: Miscellaneous

Section 1. Homestead and Exemption Laws.
The general assembly shall pass liberal homestead and exemption laws.

Section 2. Lotteries Prohibited Exceptions.

(1) The general assembly shall have no power to authorize lotteries for any purpose; except that the conducting of such games of chance as provided in subsections (2) to (4) of this section shall be lawful on and after January 1, 1959, and the conducting of state- supervised lotteries pursuant to subsection (7) of this section shall be lawful on and after January 1, 1981.
(2) No game of chance pursuant to this subsection (2) and subsections (3) and (4) of this section shall be conducted by any person, firm, or organization, unless a license as provided for in this subsection (2) has been issued to the firm or organization conducting such games of chance. The secretary of state shall, upon application therefore on such forms as shall be prescribed by the secretary of state and upon the payment of an annual fee as determined by the general assembly, issue a license for the conducting of such games of chance to any bona fide chartered branch or lodge or chapter of a national or state organization or to any bona fide religious, charitable, labor, fraternal, educational, voluntary firemen's or veterans' organization which operates without profit to its members and which has been in existence continuously for a period of five years immediately prior to the making of said application for such license and has had during the entire five--year period a dues paying membership engaged in carrying out the objects of said corporation or organization, such license to expire at the end of each calendar year in which it was issued.
(3) The license issued by the secretary of state shall authorize and permit the licensee to conduct games of chance, restricted to the selling of rights to participate and the awarding of prizes in the specific kind of game of chance commonly known as bingo or lotto, in which prizes are awarded on the basis of designated

numbers or symbols on a card conforming to numbers or symbols selected at random and in the specific game of chance commonly known as raffles, conducted by the drawing of prizes or by the allotment of prizes by chance.

(4) Such games of chance shall be subject to the following restrictions:

(a) The entire net proceeds of any game shall be exclusively devoted to the lawful purposes of organizations permitted to conduct such games.

(b) No person except a bona fide member of any organization may participate in the management or operation of any such game.

(c) No person may receive any remuneration or profit for participating in the management or operation of any such game.

(5) Subsections (2) to (4) of this section are self-enacting, but laws may be enacted supplementary to and in pursuance of, but not contrary to, the provisions thereof.

(6) The enforcement of this section shall be under such official or department of government of the state of Colorado as the general assembly shall provide.

(7) Any provision of this constitution to the contrary notwithstanding, the general assembly may establish a state-supervised lottery. Unless otherwise provided by statute, all proceeds from the lottery, after deduction of prizes and expenses, shall be allocated to the conservation trust fund of the state for distribution to municipalities and counties for park, recreation, and open space purposes.

Section 3. Arbitration Laws.

It shall be the duty of the general assembly to pass such laws as may be necessary and proper to decide differences by arbitrators, to be appointed by mutual agreement of the parties to any controversy who may choose that mode of adjustment. The powers and duties of such arbitrators shall be as prescribed by law.

Section 4. **Felony Defined.**
The term felony, wherever it may occur in this constitution, or the laws of the state, shall be construed to mean any criminal offense punishable by death or imprisonment in the penitentiary, and none other.

Section 5. **Spurious and Drugged Liquors Laws Concerning.**

Repealed.

Section 6. **Preservation of Forests.**
The general assembly shall enact laws in order to prevent the destruction of, and to keep in good preservation, the forests upon the lands of the state, or upon lands of the public domain, the control of which shall be conferred by congress upon the state.

Section 7. **Land Value Increase Arboreal Planting Exempt.**

Repealed.

Section 8. **Publication of Laws.**
The general assembly shall provide for the publication of the laws passed at each session thereof.

Section 9. **Limited Gaming Permitted.**

(1) Any provisions of section 2 of this article XVIII or any other provisions of this constitution to the contrary notwithstanding, limited gaming in the City of Central, the City of Black Hawk, and the City of Cripple Creek shall be lawful as of October 1, 1991. **(2)** The administration and regulation of this section 9 shall be under an appointed limited gaming control commission, referred to in this section 9 as the commission; said commission to be created under such official or department of government of the state of Colorado as the general assembly shall provide by May

1, 1991. Such official or the director of the department of government shall appoint the commission by July 1, 1991. The commission shall promulgate all necessary rules and regulations relating to the licensing of limited gaming by October 1, 1991, in the manner authorized by statute for the promulgation of administrative rules and regulations. Such rules and regulations shall include the necessary defining of terms that are not otherwise defined.

(3) Limited gaming shall be subject to the following:

(a) Limited gaming shall take place only in the existing Colorado cities of: the City of Central, county of Gilpin, the City of Black Hawk, county of Gilpin, and the City of Cripple Creek, county of Teller. Such limited gaming shall be further confined to the commercial districts of said cities as said districts are respectively defined in the city ordinances adopted by: the City of Central on October 7, 1981, the City of Black Hawk on May 4, 1978, and the City of Cripple Creek on December 3, 1973.

(b) Limited gaming shall only be conducted in structures which conform, as determined by the respective municipal governing bodies, to the architectural styles and designs that were common to the areas prior to World War I and which conform to the requirements of applicable respective city ordinances, regardless of the age of said structures.

(c) No more than thirty-five percent of the square footage of any building and no more than fifty percent of any one floor of such building, may be used for limited gaming.

(d) Limited gaming operations shall be prohibited between the hours of 2:00 o'clock a.m. and 8:00 o'clock a.m., unless such hours are revised as provided in subsection (7) of this section.

(e) Limited gaming may occur in establishments licensed to sell alcoholic beverages.

(4) As certain terms are used in regards to limited gaming:

(a) "Adjusted gross proceeds" means the total amount of all wagers made by players on limited gaming less all payments to players; said payments to players being deemed to include all payments of cash premiums, merchandise, tokens, redeemable game credits, or any other thing of value.

(b) "Limited gaming" means the use of slot machines and the card games of blackjack and poker, each game having a maximum single bet of five dollars, unless such games or single bets are revised as provided in subsection (7) of this section.

(c) "Slot machine" means any mechanical, electrical, video, electronic, or other device, contrivance, or machine which, after insertion of a coin, token, or similar object, or upon payment of any required consideration whatsoever by a player, is available to be played or operated, and which, whether by reason of the skill of the player or application of the element of chance, or both, may deliver or entitle the player operating the machine to receive cash premiums, merchandise, tokens, redeemable game credits, or any other thing of value other than unredeemable free games, whether the payoff is made automatically from the machines or in any other manner.

(5)(a) Up to a maximum of forty percent of the adjusted gross proceeds of limited gaming shall be paid by each licensee, in addition to any applicable license fees, for the privilege of conducting limited gaming. Subject to subsection (7) of this section, such percentage shall be established annually by the commission according to the criteria established by the general assembly in the implementing legislation to be enacted pursuant to paragraph (c) of this subsection (5). Such payments shall be made into a limited gaming fund that is hereby created in the state treasury.

(b)(I) From the moneys in the limited gaming fund, the state treasurer is hereby authorized to pay all ongoing expenses of the commission and any other state agency, related to the administration of this section 9. Such payment shall be made upon proper presentation of a voucher prepared by the commission in accordance with statutes governing payments of liabilities incurred on behalf of the state. Such payment shall not be conditioned on any appropriation by the general assembly.

(II) At the end of each state fiscal year, the state treasurer shall distribute the balance remaining in the limited gaming fund, except for an amount equal to all expenses of the administration of this section 9 for the preceding two-month period, according to the following guidelines and subject to the distribution criteria provided in subsection (7) of this section: fifty percent shall be transferred to the state general fund or such other fund as the general assembly shall provide; twenty-eight percent shall be transferred to the state historical fund, which fund is hereby created in the state treasury; twelve percent shall be distributed to the governing bodies of Gilpin county and Teller county in proportion to the gaming revenues generated in each county; the remaining ten percent shall be distributed to the governing bodies of the cities of: the City of Central, the City of Black Hawk, and the City of Cripple Creek in proportion to the gaming revenues generated in each respective city.

(III) Of the moneys in the state historical fund, from which the state treasurer shall also make annual distributions, twenty percent shall be used for the preservation and restoration of the cities of: the City of Central, the City of Black Hawk, and the City of Cripple Creek, and such moneys shall be distributed, to the governing bodies of the respective cities, according to the proportion of the gaming revenues generated in each respective city. The remaining eighty percent in the state historical fund shall be used for the historic preservation and restoration of historical sites and municipalities throughout the state in a manner to be determined by the general assembly.

(c) and (d) Repealed.

(e) The general assembly shall enact provisions for the special licensing of qualifying nonprofit charitable organizations desiring to periodically host charitable gaming activities in licensed gaming establishments.

(f) If any provision of this section 9 is held invalid, the remainder of this section 9 shall remain unimpaired.

(6) LOCAL VOTE ON LEGALITY OF LIMITED GAMING - ELECTION REQUIRED. (a) Except as provided in paragraph (e) of this subsection (6), limited gaming shall not be lawful within any city, town, or unincorporated portion of a county which has been granted constitutional authority for limited gaming within its boundaries unless first approved by an affirmative vote of a majority of the electors of such city, town, or county voting thereon. The question shall first be submitted to the electors at a general, regular, or special election held within thirteen months after the effective date of the amendment which first adds such city, county, or town to those authorized for limited gaming pursuant to this constitution; and said election shall be conducted pursuant to applicable state or local government election laws.
(b) If approval of limited gaming is not obtained when the question is first submitted to the electors, the question may be submitted at subsequent elections held in accordance with paragraph (d) of this subsection (6); except that, once approval is obtained, limited gaming shall thereafter be lawful within the said city, town, or unincorporated portion of a county so long as the city, town, or county remains among those with constitutional authority for limited gaming within their boundaries.
(c) Nothing contained in this subsection (6) shall be construed to limit the ability of a city, town, or county to regulate the conduct of limited gaming as otherwise authorized by statute or by this constitution.

(d)(I) The question submitted to the electors at any election held pursuantto this subsection (6) shall be phrased in substantially the following form: "Shall limited gaming be lawful within?"
(II) The failure to acquire approval of limited gaming in the unincorporated portion of a county shall not prevent lawful limited gaming within a city or town located in such county where such approval is acquired in a city or town election, and failure to acquire such approval in a city or town election shall not prevent lawful limited gaming within the unincorporated area of the county in which such city or town is located where such

approval is acquired in an election in the unincorporated area of a county.

(III) If approval of limited gaming is not acquired when the question is first submitted in accordance with this subsection (6), the question may be submitted at subsequent elections so long as at least four years have elapsed since any previous election at which the question was submitted.

(e) Nothing contained in this subsection (6) shall be construed to affect the authority granted upon the initial adoption of this section at the 1990 general election, or the conduct and regulation of gaming on Indian reservations pursuant to federal law.

(f) For purposes of this subsection (6), a "city, town, or county" includes all land and buildings located within, or owned and controlled by, such city, town, or county or any political subdivision thereof. "City, town, or county" also includes the city and county of Denver.

(7) LOCAL ELECTIONS TO REVISE LIMITS APPLICABLE TO GAMING - STATEWIDE ELECTIONS TO INCREASE GAMING TAXES. (a) Through local elections, the voters of the cities of Central, Black Hawk, and Cripple Creek are authorized to revise limits on gaming that apply to licensees operating in their city's gaming district to extend:

(I) Hours of limited gaming operation;
(II) Approved games to include roulette or craps, or both; and
(III) Single bets up to one hundred dollars.

(b) Limited gaming tax revenues attributable to the operation of this subsection (7) shall be deposited in the limited gaming fund. The commission shall annually determine the amount of such revenues generated in each city.

(c) From gaming tax revenues attributable to the operation of this subsection (7), the treasurer shall pay:

(I) Those ongoing expenses of the commission and other state agencies that are related to the administration of this subsection (7);

(II) Annual adjustments, in connection with distributions to limited gaming fund recipients listed in subsection (5)(b)(II) of this section, to reflect the lesser of six percent of, or the actual percentage of, annual growth in gaming tax revenues attributable to this subsection (7); and

(III) Of the remaining gaming tax revenues, distributions in the following proportions:

(A) Seventy-eight percent to the state's public community colleges, junior colleges, and local district colleges to supplement existing state funding for student financial aid programs and classroom instruction programs; provided that such revenue shall be distributed to institutions that were operating on and after January 1, 2008, in proportion to their respective full-time equivalent student enrollments in the previous fiscal year;

(B) Ten percent to the governing bodies of the cities of Central, Black Hawk, and Cripple Creek to address local gaming impacts; provided that such revenue shall be distributed based on the proportion of gaming tax revenues, attributable to the operation of this subsection (7), that are paid by licensees operating in each city; and

(C) Twelve percent to the governing bodies of Gilpin and Teller Counties to address local gaming impacts; provided that such revenue shall be distributed based on the proportion of gaming tax revenues, attributable to the operation of this subsection (7), that are paid by licensees operating in each county.

(d) After July 1, 2009, the commission shall implement revisions to limits on gaming as approved by voters in the cities of Central, Black Hawk, or Cripple Creek. The general assembly is also authorized to enact, as necessary, legislation that will facilitate the operation of this subsection (7).

(e) If local voters in one or more cities revise any limits on gaming as provided in paragraph (a) of this subsection (7), any commission action pursuant to subsection (5) of this section that increases gaming taxes from the levels imposed as of July 1,

2008, shall be effective only if approved by voters at a statewide election held under section 20(4)(a) of article X of this constitution.

(f) Gaming tax revenues attributable to the operation of this subsection (7) shall be collected and spent as a voter-approved revenue change without regard to any limitation contained in section 20 of article X of this constitution or any other law.

Section 9a. U.S. Senators and Representatives - Limitations on Terms.

(1) In order to broaden the opportunities for public service and to assure that members of the United States Congress from Colorado are representative of and responsive to Colorado citizens, no United States Senator from Colorado shall serve more than two consecutive terms in the United States Senate, and no United States Representative from Colorado shall serve more than three consecutive terms in the United States House of Representatives. This limitation on the number of terms shall apply to terms of office beginning on or after January 1, 1995. Any person appointed or elected to fill a vacancy in the United States Congress and who serves at least one half of a term of office shall be considered to have served a term in that office for purposes of this subsection (1). Terms are considered consecutive unless they are at least four years apart.

(2) The people of Colorado hereby state their support for a nationwide limit of twelve consecutive years of service in the United States Senate and six consecutive years of service in the United States House of Representatives and instruct their public officials to use their best efforts to work for such a limit.

(3) The people of Colorado declare that the provisions of this section shall be deemed severable from the remainder of this measure and that their intention is that federal officials elected from Colorado will continue voluntarily to observe the wishes of the people as stated in this section in the event any provision thereof is held invalid. The severability provisions of Section 10 of Article XVIII of the Colorado Constitution apply to this Section 9a.

Section 10. Severability of Constitutional Provisions.
If any provision of any section of any article in this constitution is found by a court of competent jurisdiction to be unconstitutional, the remaining provisions are valid unless the court holds that the valid provisions are so essentially and inseparably connected with, and so dependent upon, the void provision that it cannot be presumed the enactment of the valid provisions would have occurred without the void one; or unless the court determines that the valid provisions, standing alone, are incomplete and not capable of being executed.

Section 11. Elected Government Officials Limitation on Terms.
(1) In order to broaden the opportunities for public service and to assure that elected officials of governments are responsive to the citizens of those governments, no nonjudicial elected official of any county, city and county, city, town, school district, service authority, or any other political subdivision of the State of Colorado, no member of the state board of education, and no elected member of the governing board of a state institution of higher education shall serve more than two consecutive terms in office, except that with respect to terms of office which are two years or shorter in duration, no such elected official shall serve more than three consecutive terms in office. This limitation on the number of terms shall apply to terms of office beginning on or after January 1, 1995. For purposes of this Section 11, terms are considered consecutive unless they are at least four years apart.

(2) The voters of any such political subdivision may lengthen, shorten or eliminate the limitations on terms of office imposed by this Section 11. The voters of the state may lengthen, shorten, or eliminate the limitations on terms of office for the state board of education or the governing board of a state institution of higher education imposed by this Section 11.

(3) The provisions of this Section 11 shall apply to every home rule county, home rule city and county, home rule city and home rule town, notwithstanding any provision of Article XX, or Sections 16 and 17 of Article XIV, of the Colorado Constitution.

Section 12.

Repealed.

Section 12a Congressional Term Limits Declaration.
(1) Information for voters about candidates' decisions to term limit themselves is more important than party labeling, therefore, any candidate seeking to be elected to the United States Congress shall be allowed, but not required, to submit to the secretary of state an executed copy of the Term Limits Declaration set forth in subsection (2) of this section not later than 15 days prior to the certification of every congressional election ballot to each county clerk and recorder by the secretary of state. The secretary of state shall not refuse to place a candidate on any ballot due to the candidate's decision not to submit such declaration.
(2) The language of the Term Limits Declaration shall be as set forth herein and the secretary of state shall incorporate the applicable language in square brackets "[]" for the office the candidate seeks:
CONGRESSIONAL TERM LIMITS DECLARATION
TERM LIMITS DECLARATION ONE
PART A: I, ---------------, voluntarily declare that, if elected, I will not serve in the United States [House of Representatives more than 3 terms] [Senate more than 2 terms] after the effective date of the Congressional Term Limits Declaration Act of 1998.

Signature by candidate executes Part A Date
PART B: I, ---------------, authorize and request that the secretary of state place the applicable ballot designation, "Signed declaration to limit service to no more than [3 terms] [2 terms]" next to my name on every election ballot and in all government-sponsored voter education material in which my name appears as a candidate for the office to which Term Limit Declaration One refers.

Signature by candidate executes Part B Date
If the candidate chooses not to execute any or all parts of Term Limits Declaration One, then he or she may execute and submit to the secretary of state any or all parts of Term Limits Declaration Two.
TERM LIMITS DECLARATION TWO
PART A: I, ---------------, have voluntarily chosen not to sign Term Limits Declaration One. If I had signed that declaration, I would have voluntarily agreed to limit my service in the United States [House of Representatives to no more than 3 terms] [Senate to no more than 2 terms] after the passage of the congressional Term Limits Declaration Amendment of 1998.

Signature by candidate executes Part A Date
After executing Part A, a candidate may execute and submit the voluntary statement in Part B.
PART B: I, ---------------, authorize and request that the secretary of state place the ballot designation, "Chose not to sign declaration to limit service to [3 terms] [2 terms]" next to my name on every official election ballot and in all government-sponsored voter education material in which my name appears as a candidate for the office to which Term Limits Declaration Two refers.

Signature by candidate executes Part B Date

(3) In the ballot designations in this section, the secretary of state shall incorporate the applicable language in brackets for the office the candidate seeks. Terms shall be calculated without regard to whether the terms were served consecutively.
(4) The secretary of state shall allow any candidate who at any time has submitted an executed copy of Term Limits Declaration One or Two, to timely submit an executed copy of Term Limits Declaration One or Two at which time all provisions affecting that Term Limits Declaration shall apply.
(5) The secretary of state shall place on that part of the official election ballot and in all government-sponsored voter education material, immediately following the name of each candidate who

has executed and submitted Parts A and B of Term Limits Declaration One, the words, "Signed declaration to limit service to [3 terms] [2 terms]" unless the candidate has qualified as a candidate for a term that would exceed the number of terms set forth in Term Limits Declaration One. The secretary of state shall place on that part of the official election ballot and in all government-sponsored voter education material, immediately following the name of each candidate who has executed and submitted Parts A and B of Term Limits Declaration Two the words, "Chose not to sign declaration to limit service to [3 terms] [2 terms]".

(6) For the purpose of this section, service in office for more than one-half of a term shall be deemed as service for a full term.

(7) No candidate shall have more than one declaration and ballot designation in effect for any office at the same time and a candidate may only execute and submit Part B of a declaration if Part A of that declaration is or has been executed and submitted.

(8) The secretary of state shall provide candidates with all the declarations in this section and promulgate regulations as provided by law to facilitate implementation of this section as long as the regulations do not alter the intent of this section.

(9) If any portion of this section be adjudicated invalid, the remaining portion shall be severed from the invalid portion to the greatest possible extent and be given the fullest force and application.

Section 12b. Prohibited Methods of Taking Wildlife.

(1) It shall be unlawful to take wildlife with any leghold trap, any instant kill body-gripping design trap, or by poison or snare in the state of Colorado.

(2) The provisions of subsection (1) of this section shall not prohibit:

(a) The taking of wildlife by use of the devices or methods described in subsection (1) of this section by federal, state, county, or municipal departments of health for the purpose of protecting human health or safety;

(b) The use of the devices or methods described in subsection

(1) of this section for controlling:
(I) wild or domestic rodents, except for beaver or muskrat, as otherwise authorized by law; or
(II) wild or domestic birds as otherwise authorized by law;

(c) The use of non-lethal snares, traps specifically designed not to kill, or nets to take wildlife for scientific research projects, for falconry, for relocation, or for medical treatment pursuant to regulations established by the Colorado wildlife commission; or
(d) The use of traps, poisons or nets by the Colorado division of wildlife to take or manage fish or other non-mammalian aquatic wildlife.

(3) Notwithstanding the provisions of this section 12, the owner or lessee of private property primarily used for commercial livestock or crop production, or the employees of such owner or lessee, shall not be prohibited from using the devices or methods described in subsection (1) of this section on such private property so long as:

(a) such use does not exceed one thirty day period per year; and
(b) the owner or lessee can present on-site evidence to the division of wildlife that ongoing damage to livestock or crops has not been alleviated by the use of non-lethal or lethal control methods which are not prohibited.

(4) The provisions of this section 12 shall not apply to the taking of wildlife with firearms, fishing equipment, archery equipment, or other implements in hand as authorized by law.
(5) The general assembly shall enact, amend, or repeal such laws as are necessary to implement the provisions of this section As used in this section, unless the context otherwise requires:

(a) The term "taking" shall be defined as provided in section 33-1-102 (43), C.R.S., on the date this section is enacted.

(b) The term "wildlife" shall be defined as provided in section 33-1-102 (51), C.R.S., on the date this section is enacted.

Section 13. Medical use of marijuana for persons suffering from debilitating medical conditions.

(1) As used in this section, these terms are defined as follows:

(a) "Debilitating medical condition" means:

(I) Cancer, glaucoma, positive status for human immunodeficiency virus, or acquired immune deficiency syndrome, or treatment for such conditions;

(II) A chronic or debilitating disease or medical condition, or treatment for such conditions, which produces, for a specific patient, one or more of the following, and for which, in the professional opinion of the patient's physician, such condition or conditions reasonably may be alleviated by the medical use of marijuana: cachexia; severe pain; severe nausea; seizures, including those that are characteristic of epilepsy; or persistent muscle spasms, including those that are characteristic of multiple sclerosis; or

(III) Any other medical condition, or treatment for such condition, approved by the state health agency, pursuant to its rule making authority or its approval of any petition submitted by a patient or physician as provided in this section.

(b) "Medical use" means the acquisition, possession, production, use, or transportation of marijuana or paraphernalia related to the administration of such marijuana to address the symptoms or effects of a patient's debilitating medical condition, which may be authorized only after a diagnosis of the patient's debilitating medical condition by a physician or physicians, as provided by this section.

(c) "Parent" means a custodial mother or father of a patient under the age of eighteen years, any person having custody of a patient under the age of eighteen years, or any person serving as a legal guardian for a patient under the age of eighteen years.

(d) "Patient" means a person who has a debilitating medical condition.

(e) "Physician" means a doctor of medicine who maintains, in good standing, a license to practice medicine issued by the state of Colorado.

(f) "Primary care-giver" means a person, other than the patient and the patient's physician, who is eighteen years of age or older and has significant responsibility for managing the well-being of a patient who has a debilitating medical condition.

(g) "Registry identification card" means that document, issued by the state health agency, which identifies a patient authorized to engage in the medical use of marijuana and such patient's primary care-giver, if any has been designated.

(h) "State health agency" means that public health related entity of state government designated by the governor to establish and maintain a confidential registry of patients authorized to engage in the medical use of marijuana and enact rules to administer this program.

(i) "Usable form of marijuana" means the seeds, leaves, buds, and flowers of the plant (genus) cannabis, and any mixture or preparation thereof, which are appropriate for medical use as provided in this section, but excludes the plant's stalks, stems, and roots.

(j) "Written documentation" means a statement signed by a patient's physician or copies of the patient's pertinent medical records.

(2)(a) Except as otherwise provided in subsections (5), (6), and (8) of this section, a patient or primary care-giver charged with a violation of the state's criminal laws related to the patient's medical use of marijuana will be deemed to have established an affirmative defense to such allegation where:

(I) The patient was previously diagnosed by a physician as having a debilitating medical condition;

(II) The patient was advised by his or her physician, in the context of a bona fide physician-patient relationship, that the patient might benefit from the medical use of marijuana in connection with a debilitating medical condition; and
(III) The patient and his or her primary care-giver were collectively in possession of amounts of marijuana only as permitted under this section.
This affirmative defense shall not exclude the assertion of any other defense where a patient or primary care-giver is charged with a violation of state law related to the patient's medical use of marijuana.

(b) Effective June 1, 1999, it shall be an exception from the state's criminal laws for any patient or primary care-giver in lawful possession of a registry identification card to engage or assist in the medical use of marijuana, except as otherwise provided in subsections (5) and (8) of this section.
(c) It shall be an exception from the state's criminal laws for any physician to:

(I) Advise a patient whom the physician has diagnosed as having a debilitating medical condition, about the risks and benefits of medical use of marijuana or that he or she might benefit from the medical use of marijuana, provided that such advice is based upon the physician's contemporaneous assessment of the patient's medical history and current medical condition and a bona fide physician-patient relationship; or
(II) Provide a patient with written documentation, based upon the physician's contemporaneous assessment of the patient's medical history and current medical condition and a bona fide physician-patient relationship, stating that the patient has a debilitating medical condition and might benefit from the medical use of marijuana.
No physician shall be denied any rights or privileges for the acts authorized by this subsection.

(d) Notwithstanding the foregoing provisions, no person, including a patient or primary care-giver, shall be entitled to the protection of this section for his or her acquisition, possession, manufacture, production, use, sale, distribution, dispensing, or transportation of marijuana for any use other than medical use.
(e) Any property interest that is possessed, owned, or used in connection with the medical use of marijuana or acts incidental to such use, shall not be harmed, neglected, injured, or destroyed while in the possession of state or local law enforcement officials where such property has been seized in connection with the claimed medical use of marijuana. Any such property interest shall not be forfeited under any provision of state law providing for the forfeiture of property other than as a sentence imposed after conviction of a criminal offense or entry of a plea of guilty to such offense. Marijuana and paraphernalia seized by state or local law enforcement officials from a patient or primary care-giver in connection with the claimed medical use of marijuana shall be returned immediately upon the determination of the district attorney or his or her designee that the patient or primary care-giver is entitled to the protection contained in this section as may be evidenced, for example, by a decision not to prosecute, the dismissal of charges, or acquittal.

(3) The state health agency shall create and maintain a confidential registry of patients who have applied for and are entitled to receive a registry identification card according to the criteria set forth in this subsection, effective June 1, 1999.

(a) No person shall be permitted to gain access to any information about patients in the state health agency's confidential registry, or any information otherwise maintained by the state health agency about physicians and primary care-givers, except for authorized employees of the state health agency in the course of their official duties and authorized employees of state or local law enforcement agencies which have stopped or arrested a person who claims to be engaged in the medical use of marijuana and in possession of a registry identification card or its functional equivalent, pursuant to paragraph (e) of this subsection (3). Authorized employees of state or local law enforcement agencies shall be granted access to the information contained within the state health agency's confidential registry only for the purpose of verifying that an individual who has presented a registry identification card to a state or local law enforcement official is lawfully in possession of such card.

(b) In order to be placed on the state's confidential registry for the medical use of marijuana, a patient must reside in Colorado and submit the completed application form adopted by the state health agency, including the following information, to the state health agency:

(I) The original or a copy of written documentation stating that the patient has been diagnosed with a debilitating medical condition and the physician's conclusion that the patient might benefit from the medical use of marijuana;

(II) The name, address, date of birth, and social security number of the patient;

(III) The name, address, and telephone number of the patient's physician; and

(IV) The name and address of the patient's primary care-giver, if one is designated at the time of application.

(c) Within thirty days of receiving the information referred to in subparagraphs (3) (b) (I)-(IV), the state health agency shall verify medical information contained in the patient's written documentation. The agency shall notify the applicant that his or her application for a registry identification card has been denied if the agency's review of such documentation discloses that: the information required pursuant to paragraph (3) (b) of this section has not been provided or has been falsified; the documentation fails to state that the patient has a debilitating medical condition specified in this section or by state health agency rule; or the physician does not have a license to practice medicine issued by the state of Colorado. Otherwise, not more than five days after verifying such information, the state health agency shall issue one serially numbered registry identification card to the patient, stating:

(I) The patient's name, address, date of birth, and social security number;
(II) That the patient's name has been certified to the state health agency as a person who has a debilitating medical condition, whereby the patient may address such condition with the medical use of marijuana;
(III) The date of issuance of the registry identification card and the date of expiration of such card, which shall be one year from the date of issuance; and
(IV) The name and address of the patient's primary care-giver, if any is designated at the time of application.

(d) Except for patients applying pursuant to subsection (6) of this section, where the state health agency, within thirty-five days of receipt of an application, fails to issue a registry identification card or fails to issue verbal or written notice of denial of such application, the patient's application for such card will be deemed to have been approved. Receipt shall be deemed to have occurred upon delivery to the state health agency, or deposit in the United States mails. Notwithstanding the foregoing, no application shall be deemed received prior to June 1, 1999. A patient who is questioned by any state or local law enforcement official about his or her medical use of marijuana shall provide a copy of the application submitted to the state health agency, including the written documentation and proof of the date of mailing or other transmission of the written documentation for delivery to the state health agency, which shall be accorded the same legal effect as a registry identification card, until such time as the patient receives notice that the application has been denied.
(e) A patient whose application has been denied by the state health agency may not reapply during the six months following the date of the denial and may not use an application for a registry identification card as provided in paragraph (3) (d) of this section. The denial of a registry identification card shall be considered a final agency action. Only the patient whose

application has been denied shall have standing to contest the agency action.

(f) When there has been a change in the name, address, physician, or primary care- giver of a patient who has qualified for a registry identification card, that patient must notify the state health agency of any such change within ten days. A patient who has not designated a primary care-giver at the time of application to the state health agency may do so in writing at any time during the effective period of the registry identification card, and the primary care-giver may act in this capacity after such designation. To maintain an effective registry identification card, a patient must annually resubmit, at least thirty days prior to the expiration date stated on the registry identification card, updated written documentation to the state health agency, as well as the name and address of the patient's primary care-giver, if any is designated at such time.

(g) Authorized employees of state or local law enforcement agencies shall immediately notify the state health agency when any person in possession of a registry identification card has been determined by a court of law to have willfully violated the provisions of this section or its implementing legislation, or has pled guilty to such offense.

(h) A patient who no longer has a debilitating medical condition shall return his or her registry identification card to the state health agency within twenty-four hours of receiving such diagnosis by his or her physician.

(i) The state health agency may determine and levy reasonable fees to pay for any direct or indirect administrative costs associated with its role in this program.

(4)(a) A patient may engage in the medical use of marijuana, with no more marijuana than is medically necessary to address a debilitating medical condition. A patient's medical use of marijuana, within the following limits, is lawful:

(I) No more than two ounces of a usable form of marijuana; and

(II) No more than six marijuana plants, with three or fewer being mature, flowering plants that are producing a usable form of marijuana.

(b) For quantities of marijuana in excess of these amounts, a patient or his or her primary care-giver may raise as an affirmative defense to charges of violation of state law that such greater amounts were medically necessary to address the patient's debilitating medical condition.

(5)(a) No patient shall:

(I) Engage in the medical use of marijuana in a way that endangers the health or well-being of any person; or
(II) Engage in the medical use of marijuana in plain view of, or in a place open to, the general public.

(b) In addition to any other penalties provided by law, the state health agency shall revoke for a period of one year the registry identification card of any patient found to have willfully violated the provisions of this section or the implementing legislation adopted by the general assembly.

(6) Notwithstanding paragraphs (2) (a) and (3) (d) of this section, no patient under eighteen years of age shall engage in the medical use of marijuana unless:
(a) Two physicians have diagnosed the patient as having a debilitating medical condition;

(b) One of the physicians referred to in paragraph (6) (a) has explained the possible risks and benefits of medical use of marijuana to the patient and each of the patient's parents residing in Colorado;
(c) The physicians referred to in paragraph (6) (b) has provided the patient with the written documentation, specified in subparagraph (3) (b) (I);
(d) Each of the patient's parents residing in Colorado consent in writing to the state health agency to permit the patient to

engage in the medical use of marijuana;
(e) A parent residing in Colorado consents in writing to serve as a patient's primary care-giver;
(f) A parent serving as a primary care-giver completes and submits an application for a registry identification card as provided in subparagraph (3) (b) of this section and the written consents referred to in paragraph (6) (d) to the state health agency;
(g) The state health agency approves the patient's application and transmits the patient's registry identification card to the parent designated as a primary care-giver;
(h) The patient and primary care-giver collectively possess amounts of marijuana no greater than those specified in subparagraph (4) (a) (I) and (II); and
(i) The primary care-giver controls the acquisition of such marijuana and the dosage and frequency of its use by the patient.

(7) Not later than March 1, 1999, the governor shall designate, by executive order, the state health agency as defined in paragraph (1) (g) of this section.
(8) Not later than April 30, 1999, the General Assembly shall define such terms and enact such legislation as may be necessary for implementation of this section, as well as determine and enact criminal penalties for:

(a) Fraudulent representation of a medical condition by a patient to a physician, state health agency, or state or local law enforcement official for the purpose of falsely obtaining a registry identification card or avoiding arrest and prosecution;
(b) Fraudulent use or theft of any person's registry identification card to acquire, possess, produce, use, sell, distribute, or transport marijuana, including but not limited to cards that are required to be returned where patients are no longer diagnosed as having a debilitating medical condition;
(c) Fraudulent production or counterfeiting of, or tampering with, one or more registry identification cards; or
(d) Breach of confidentiality of information provided to or by the

state health agency.

(9) Not later than June 1, 1999, the state health agency shall develop and make available to residents of Colorado an application form for persons seeking to be listed on the confidential registry of patients. By such date, the state health agency shall also enact rules of administration, including but not limited to rules governing the establishment and confidentiality of the registry, the verification of medical information, the issuance and form of registry identification cards, communications with law enforcement officials about registry identification cards that have been suspended where a patient is no longer diagnosed as having a debilitating medical condition, and the manner in which the agency may consider adding debilitating medical conditions to the list provided in this section. Beginning June 1, 1999, the state health agency shall accept physician or patient initiated petitions to add debilitating medical conditions to the list provided in this section and, after such hearing as the state health agency deems appropriate, shall approve or deny such petitions within one hundred eighty days of submission. The decision to approve or deny a petition shall be considered a final agency action.

(10)(a) No governmental, private, or any other health insurance provider shall be required to be liable for any claim for reimbursement for the medical use of marijuana.

(b) Nothing in this section shall require any employer to accommodate the medical use of marijuana in any work place.

(11) Unless otherwise provided by this section, all provisions of this section shall become effective upon official declaration of the vote hereon by proclamation of the governor, pursuant to article V, section (1) (4), and shall apply to acts or offenses committed on or after that date.

Section 15. **State minimum wage rate**

Effective January 1, 2017, Colorado's minimum wage is increased to $9.30 per hour and is increased annually by 0.90 each January 1 until it reaches $12 per hour effective January 2020, and thereafter is adjusted annually for cost of living increases, as measured by the Consumer Price Index used for Colorado. This minimum wage shall be paid to employees who receive the state or federal minimum wage. No more than $3.02 per hour in tip income may be used to offset the minimum wage of employees who regularly receive tips.

Section 16. (1) PURPOSE AND FINDINGS.

(a) In the interest of the efficient use of law enforcement resources, enhancing revenue for public purposes, and individual freedom, the people of the state of Colorado find and declare that the use of marijuana should be legal for persons twenty-one years of age or older and taxed in a manner similar to alcohol.

(b) In the interest of the health and public safety of our citizenry, the people of the state of Colorado further find and declare that marijuana should be regulated in a manner similar to alcohol so that:

(I) Individuals will have to show proof of age before purchasing marijuana;
(II) Selling, distributing, or transferring marijuana to minors and other individuals under the age of twenty-one shall remain illegal;
(III) Driving under the influence of marijuana shall remain illegal;
(IV) Legitimate, taxpaying business people, and not criminal actors, will conduct sales of marijuana; and
(V) Marijuana sold in this state will be labeled and subject to additional regulations to ensure that consumers are informed and protected.

(c) In the interest of enacting rational policies for the treatment of all variations of the cannabis plant, the people of Colorado further find and declare that industrial hemp should be regulated separately from strains of cannabis with higher delta-9 tetrahydrocannabinol (THC) concentrations.

(d) The people of the state of Colorado further find and declare that it is necessary to ensure consistency and fairness in the application of this section throughout the state and that, therefore, the matters addressed by this section are, except as specified herein, matters of statewide concern.

(2) DEFINITIONS. As used in this section, unless the context otherwise requires,

(a) "Colorado Medical Marijuana Code" means article 43.3 of title 12, Colorado Revised Statutes.

(b) "Consumer" means a person twenty-one years of age or older who purchases marijuana or marijuana products for personal use by persons twenty-one years of age or older, but not for resale to others.

(c) "Department" means the department of revenue or its successor agency.

(d) "Industrial hemp" means the plant of the genus cannabis and any part of such plant, whether growing or not, with a delta-9 tetrahydrocannabinol concentration that does not exceed three-tenths percent on a dry weight basis.

(e) "Locality" means a county, municipality, or city and county.

(f) "Marijuana" or "marihuana" means all parts of the plant of the genus cannabis whether growing or not, the seeds thereof, the resin extracted from any part of the plant, and every compound, manufacture, salt, derivative, mixture, or preparation of the plant, its seeds, or its resin, including marihuana concentrate. "Marijuana" or "marihuana" does not include industrial hemp, nor does it include fiber produced from the stalks, oil, or cake made from the seeds of the plant, sterilized seed of the plant which is incapable of germination, or the weight of any other ingredient combined with marijuana to prepare topical or oral administrations, food, drink, or other product.

(g) "Marijuana accessories" means any equipment, products, or materials of any kind which are used, intended for use, or designed for use in planting, propagating, cultivating, growing, harvesting, composting, manufacturing, compounding, converting, producing, processing, preparing, testing, analyzing, packaging, repackaging, storing, vaporizing, or containing marijuana, or for ingesting, inhaling, or otherwise introducing marijuana into the human body.

(h) "Marijuana cultivation facility" means an entity licensed to cultivate, prepare, and package marijuana and sell marijuana to retail marijuana stores, to marijuana product manufacturing facilities, and to other marijuana cultivation facilities, but not to consumers.

(i) "Marijuana establishment" means a marijuana cultivation facility, a marijuana testing facility, a marijuana product manufacturing facility, or a retail marijuana store.

(j) "Marijuana product manufacturing facility" means an entity licensed to purchase marijuana; manufacture, prepare, and package marijuana products; and sell marijuana and marijuana products to other marijuana product manufacturing facilities and to retail marijuana stores, but not to consumers.

(k) "Marijuana products" means concentrated marijuana products and marijuana products that are comprised of marijuana and other ingredients and are intended for use or consumption, such as, but not limited to, edible products, ointments, and tinctures.

(l) "Marijuana testing facility" means an entity licensed to analyze and certify the safety and potency of marijuana.

(m) "Medical marijuana center" means an entity licensed by a state agency to sell marijuana and marijuana products pursuant to section 14 of this article and the Colorado Medical Marijuana Code.

(n) "Retail marijuana store" means an entity licensed topurchase marijuana from marijuana cultivation facilities and marijuana and marijuana products from marijuana product manufacturing facilities and to sell marijuana and marijuana products to consumers.

(o) "Unreasonably impracticable" means that the measures necessary to comply with the regulations require such a high investment of risk, money, time, or any other resource or asset that the operation of a marijuana establishment is not worthy of being carried out in practice by a reasonably prudent businessperson.

(3) PERSONAL USE OF MARIJUANA. Notwithstanding any other provision of law, the following acts are not unlawful and shall not be an offense under Colorado law or the law of any locality within Colorado or be a basis for seizure or forfeiture of assets under Colorado law for persons twenty-one years of age or older:

(a) Possessing, using, displaying, purchasing, or transporting marijuana accessories or one ounce or less of marijuana.
(b) Possessing, growing, processing, or transporting no more than six marijuana plants, with three or fewer being mature, flowering plants, and possession of the marijuana produced by the plants on the premises where the plants were grown, provided that the growing takes place in an enclosed, locked space, is not conducted openly or publicly, and is not made available for sale.
(c) Transfer of one ounce or less of marijuana without remuneration to a person who is twenty-one years of age or older.
(d) Consumption of marijuana, provided that nothing in this section shall permit consumption that is conducted openly and publicly or in a manner that endangers others.
(e) Assisting another person who is twenty-one years of age or older in any of the acts described in paragraphs (a) through (d) of this subsection.

(4) LAWFUL OPERATION OF MARIJUANA-RELATED FACILITIES. Notwithstanding any other provision of law, the following acts are not unlawful and shall not be an offense under Colorado law or be a basis for seizure or forfeiture of assets under Colorado law for persons twenty-one years of age or older:

(a) Manufacture, possession, or purchase of marijuana accessories or the sale of marijuana accessories to a person who is twenty-one years of age or older.
(b) Possessing, displaying, or transporting marijuana or marijuana products; purchase of marijuana from a marijuana cultivation facility; purchase of marijuana or marijuana products from a marijuana product manufacturing facility; or sale of marijuana or marijuana products to consumers, if the person conducting the activities described in this paragraph has obtained a current, valid license to operate a retail marijuana store or is acting in his or her capacity as an owner, employee or agent of a licensed retail marijuana store.
(c) Cultivating, harvesting, processing, packaging, transporting, displaying, or possessing marijuana; delivery or transfer of marijuana to a marijuana testing facility; selling marijuana to a marijuana cultivation facility, a marijuana product manufacturing facility, or a retail marijuana store; or the purchase of marijuana from a marijuana cultivation facility, if the person conducting the activities described in this paragraph has obtained a current, valid license to operate a marijuana cultivation facility or is acting in his or her capacity as an owner, employee, or agent of a licensed marijuana cultivation facility.
(d) Packaging, processing, transporting, manufacturing, displaying, or possessing marijuana or marijuana products; delivery or transfer of marijuana or marijuana products to a marijuana testing facility; selling marijuana or marijuana products to a retail marijuana store or a marijuana product manufacturing facility; the purchase of marijuana from a marijuana cultivation facility; or the purchase of marijuana or marijuana products from a marijuana product manufacturing facility, if the person conducting the activities described in this paragraph has obtained a current, valid license to operate a marijuana product manufacturing facility or is acting in his or her capacity as an owner, employee, or agent of a licensed marijuana product manufacturing facility.
(e) Possessing, cultivating, processing, repackaging, storing, transporting, displaying, transferring or delivering marijuana or marijuana products if the person has obtained a current, valid

license to operate a marijuana testing facility or is acting in his or her capacity as an owner, employee, or agent of a licensed marijuana testing facility.
(f) Leasing or otherwise allowing the use of property owned, occupied or controlled by any person, corporation or other entity for any of the activities conducted lawfully in accordance with paragraphs (a) through (e) of this subsection.

(5) REGULATION OF MARIJUANA.

(a) Not later than July 1, 2013, the department shall adopt regulations necessary for implementation of this section. Such regulations shall not prohibit the operation of marijuana establishments, either expressly or through regulations that make their operation unreasonably impracticable. Such regulations shall include:

(I) Procedures for the issuance, renewal, suspension, and revocation of a license to operate a marijuana establishment, with such procedures subject to all requirements of article 4 of title 24 of the Colorado Administrative Procedure Act or any successor provision;
(II) A schedule of application, licensing and renewal fees, provided, application fees shall not exceed five thousand dollars, with this upper limit adjusted annually for inflation, unless the department determines a greater fee is necessary to carry out its responsibilities under this section, and provided further, an entity that is licensed under the Colorado Medical Marijuana Code to cultivate or sell marijuana or to manufacture marijuana products at the time this section takes effect and that chooses to apply for a separate marijuana establishment license shall not be required to pay an application fee greater than five hundred dollars to apply for a license to operate a marijuana establishment in accordance with the provisions of this section;
(III) Qualifications for licensure that are directly and demonstrably related to the operation of a marijuana establishment;
(IV) Security requirements for marijuana establishments;

(V) Requirements to prevent the sale or diversion of marijuana and marijuana products to persons under the age of twenty-one;
(VI) Labeling requirements for marijuana and marijuana products sold or distributed by a marijuana establishment;
(VII) Health and safety regulations and standards for the manufacture of marijuana products and the cultivation of marijuana;
(VIII) Restrictions on the advertising and display of marijuana and marijuana products; and
(IX) Civil penalties for the failure to comply with regulations made pursuant to this section.

(b) In order to ensure the most secure, reliable, and accountable system for the production and distribution of marijuana and marijuana products in accordance with this subsection, in any competitive application process the department shall have as a primary consideration whether an applicant:

(I) Has prior experience producing or distributing marijuana or marijuana products pursuant to section 14 of this article and the Colorado Medical Marijuana Code in the locality in which the applicant seeks to operate a marijuana establishment; and
(II) Has, during the experience described in subparagraph (I), complied consistently with section 14 of this article, the provisions of the Colorado Medical Marijuana Code and conforming regulations.

(c) In order to ensure that individual privacy is protected, notwithstanding paragraph (a), the department shall not require a consumer to provide a retail marijuana store with personal information other than government-issued identification to determine the consumer's age, and a retail marijuana store shall not be required to acquire and record personal information about consumers other than information typically acquired in a financial transaction conducted at a retail liquor store.
(d) The general assembly shall enact an excise tax to be levied upon marijuana sold or otherwise transferred by a marijuana cultivation facility to a marijuana product manufacturing facility

or to a retail marijuana store at a rate not to exceed fifteen percent prior to January 1, 2017 and at a rate to be determined by the general assembly thereafter, and shall direct the department to establish procedures for the collection of all taxes levied. Provided, the first forty million dollars in revenue raised annually from any such excise tax shall be credited to the Public School Capital Construction Assistance Fund created by article 43.7 of title 22, C.R.S., or any successor fund dedicated to a similar purpose. Provided further, no such excise tax shall be levied upon marijuana intended for sale at medical marijuana centers pursuant to section 14 of this article and the Colorado Medical Marijuana Code.

(e) Not later than October 1, 2013, each locality shall enact an ordinance or regulation specifying the entity within the locality that is responsible for processing applications submitted for a license to operate a marijuana establishment within the boundaries of the locality and for the issuance of such licenses should the issuance by the locality become necessary because of a failure by the department to adopt regulations pursuant to paragraph (a) or because of a failure by the department to process and issue licenses as required by paragraph (g).

(f) A locality may enact ordinances or regulations, not in conflict with this section or with regulations or legislation enacted pursuant to this section, governing the time, place, manner and number of marijuana establishment operations; establishing procedures for the issuance, suspension, and revocation of a license issued by the locality in accordance with paragraph (h) or (i), such procedures to be subject to all requirements of article 4 of title 24 of the Colorado Administrative Procedure Act or any successor provision; establishing a schedule of annual operating, licensing, and application fees for marijuana establishments, provided, the application fee shall only be due if an application is submitted to a locality in accordance with paragraph (i) and a licensing fee shall only be due if a license is issued by a locality in accordance with paragraph (h) or (i); and establishing civil penalties for violation of an ordinance or regulation governing the time, place, and manner of a marijuana establishment that may operate in such locality. A locality may prohibit the operation of marijuana cultivation facilities, marijuana product manufacturing facilities, marijuana testing facilities, or retail marijuana stores through the enactment of an ordinance or through an initiated or referred measure; provided, any initiated or referred measure to prohibit the operation of marijuana cultivation facilities, marijuana product manufacturing facilities, marijuana testing facilities, or retail marijuana stores must appear on a general election ballot during an even numbered year.

(g) Each application for an annual license to operate a marijuana establishment shall be submitted to the department. The department shall:

(I) Begin accepting and processing applications on October 1, 2013;

(II) Immediately forward a copy of each application and half of the license application fee to the locality in which the applicant desires to operate the marijuana establishment;

(III) Issue an annual license to the applicant between forty-five and ninety days after receipt of an application unless the department finds the applicant is not in compliance with regulations enacted pursuant to paragraph (a) or the department is notified by the relevant locality that the applicant is not in compliance with ordinances and regulations made pursuant to paragraph (f) and in effect at the time of application, provided, where a locality has enacted a numerical limit on the number of marijuana establishments and a greater number of applicants seek licenses, the department shall solicit and consider input from the locality as to the locality's preference or preferences for licensure; and

(IV) Upon denial of an application, notify the applicant in writing of the specific reason for its denial.

(h) If the department does not issue a license to an applicant within ninety days of receipt of the application filed in accordance with paragraph (g) and does not notify the applicant of the specific reason for its denial, in writing and within such time period, or if the department has adopted regulations pursuant to paragraph (a) and has accepted applications pursuant to paragraph (g) but has not issued any licenses by January 1, 2014, the applicant may resubmit its application directly to the locality, pursuant to paragraph (e), and the locality may issue an annual license to the applicant. A locality issuing a license to an applicant shall do so within ninety days of receipt of the resubmitted application unless the locality finds and notifies the applicant that the applicant is not in compliance with ordinances and regulations made pursuant to paragraph (f) in effect at the time the application is resubmitted and the locality shall notify the department if an annual license has been issued to the applicant. If an application is submitted to a locality under this paragraph, the department shall forward to the locality the application fee paid by the applicant to the department upon request by the locality. A license issued by a locality in accordance with this paragraph shall have the same force and effect as a license issued by the department in accordance with paragraph (g) and the holder of such license shall not be subject to regulation or enforcement by the department during the term of that license. A subsequent or renewed license may be issued under this paragraph on an annual basis only upon resubmission to the locality of a new application submitted to the department pursuant to paragraph (g). Nothing in this paragraph shall limit such relief as may be available to an aggrieved party under section 24-4-104, C.R.S., of the Colorado Administrative Procedure Act or any successor provision.

(i) If the department does not adopt regulations required byparagraph (a), an applicant may submit an application directly to a locality after October 1, 2013 and the locality may issue an annual license to the applicant. A locality issuing a license to an applicant shall do so within ninety days of receipt of the application unless it finds and notifies the applicant that the applicant is not in compliance with ordinances and regulations made pursuant to paragraph (f) in effect at the time of application and shall notify the department if an annual license has been issued to the applicant. A license issued by a locality in accordance with this paragraph shall have the same force and effect as a license issued by the department in accordance with

paragraph (g) and the holder of such license shall not be subject to regulation or enforcement by the department during the term of that license. A subsequent or renewed license may be issued under this paragraph on an annual basis if the department has not adopted regulations required by paragraph (a) at least ninety days prior to the date upon which such subsequent or renewed license would be effective or if the department has adopted regulations pursuant to paragraph (a) but has not, at least ninety days after the adoption of such regulations, issued licenses pursuant to paragraph (g).
(j) Not later than July 1, 2014, the general assembly shall enact legislation governing the cultivation, processing and sale of industrial hemp.

(6) EMPLOYERS, DRIVING, MINORS AND CONTROL OF PROPERTY.(a) Nothing in this section is intended to require an employer to permit or accommodate the use, consumption, possession, transfer, display, transportation, sale or growing of marijuana in the workplace or to affect the ability of employers to have policies restricting the use of marijuana by employees.
(b) Nothing in this section is intended to allow driving under the influence of marijuana or driving while impaired by marijuana or to supersede statutory laws related to driving under the influence of marijuana or driving while impaired by marijuana, nor shall this section prevent the state from enacting and imposing penalties for driving under the influence of or while impaired by marijuana.
(c) Nothing in this section is intended to permit the transfer of marijuana, with or without remuneration, to a person under the age of twenty-one or to allow a person under the age of twenty-one to purchase, possess, use, transport, grow, or consume marijuana.
(d) Nothing in this section shall prohibit a person, employer, school, hospital, detention facility, corporation or any other entity who occupies, owns or controls a property from prohibiting or otherwise regulating the possession, consumption, use, display, transfer, distribution, sale, transportation, or growing of marijuana on or in that property.

(7) MEDICAL MARIJUANA PROVISIONS UNAFFECTED.
Nothing in this section shall be construed:

(a) To limit any privileges or rights of a medical marijuana patient, primary caregiver, or licensed entity as provided in section 14 of this article and the Colorado Medical Marijuana Code;
(b) To permit a medical marijuana center to distribute marijuana to a person who is not a medical marijuana patient;
(c) To permit a medical marijuana center to purchase marijuana or marijuana products in a manner or from a source not authorized under the Colorado Medical Marijuana Code;
(d) To permit any medical marijuana center licensed pursuant to section 14 of this article and the Colorado Medical Marijuana Code to operate on the same premises as a retail marijuana store; or
(e) To discharge the department, the Colorado Board of Health, or the Colorado Department of Public Health and Environment from their statutory and constitutional duties to regulate medical marijuana pursuant to section 14 of this article and the Colorado Medical Marijuana Code.

(8) SELF-EXECUTING, SEVERABILITY, CONFLICTING PROVISIONS. All provisions of this section are self-executing except as specified herein, are severable, and, except where otherwise indicated in the text, shall supersede conflicting state statutory, local charter, ordinance, or resolution, and other state and local provisions.

(9) EFFECTIVE DATE. Unless otherwise provided by this section, all provisions of this section shall become effective upon official declaration of the vote hereon by proclamation of the governor, pursuant to section 1(4) of article V.

Article XIX: Amendments

Section 1. Constitutional convention - how called
The general assembly may at any time by a vote of two-thirds of the members elected to each house, recommend to the electors of the state, to vote at the next general election for or against a convention to revise, alter and amend this constitution; and if a majority of those voting on the question shall declare in favor of such convention, the general assembly shall, at its next session, provide for the calling thereof. The number of members of the convention shall be twice that of the senate and they shall be elected in the same manner, at the same places, and in the same districts. The general assembly shall, in the act calling the convention, designate the day, hour and place of its meeting; fix the pay of its members and officers, and provide for the payment of the same, together with the necessary expenses of the convention. Before proceeding, the members shall take an oath to support the constitution of the United States, and of the state of Colorado, and to faithfully discharge their duties as members of the convention. The qualifications of members shall be the same as of members of the senate; and vacancies occurring shall be filled in the manner provided for filling vacancies in the general assembly. Said convention shall meet within three months after such election and prepare such revisions, alterations or amendments to the constitution as may be deemed necessary; which shall be submitted to the electors for their ratification or rejection at an election appointed by the convention for that purpose, not less than two nor more than six months after adjournment thereof; and unless so submitted and approved by a majority of the electors voting at the election, no such revision, alteration or amendment shall take effect.

Section 2. Amendments to constitution - how adopted
(1) (a) Any amendment or amendments to this constitution may be proposed in either house of the general assembly, and, if the same shall be voted for by two-thirds of all the members elected to each house, such proposed amendment or amendments, together with the ayes and noes of each house thereon, shall be

entered in full on their respective journals. The proposed amendment or amendments shall be published with the laws of that session of the general assembly. At the next general election for members of the general assembly, the said amendment or amendments shall be submitted to the registered electors of the state for their approval or rejection, and such as are approved by a majority of those voting thereon or, if applicable the number of votes required pursuant to paragraph (b) of this subsection (1), shall become part of this constitution.

(b) In order to make it more difficult to amend this constitution, a constitutional amendment shall not become part of this constitution unless the amendment is approved by at least fifty-five percent of the votes cast thereon; except that this paragraph (b) shall not apply to a constitutional amendment that is limited to repealing, in whole or in part, any provision of this constitution.

(2) If more than one amendment be submitted at any general election, each of said amendments shall be voted upon separately and votes thereon cast shall be separately counted the same as though but one amendment was submitted; but each general assembly shall have no power to propose amendments to more than six articles of this constitution.

(3) No measure proposing an amendment or amendments to this constitution shall be submitted by the general assembly to the registered electors of the state containing more than one subject, which shall be clearly expressed in its title; but if any subject shall be embraced in any measure which shall not be expressed in the title, such measure shall be void only as to so much thereof as shall not be so expressed.

Article XX: Home Rule Cities and Towns

Section 1. Incorporated
The municipal corporation known as the city of Denver and all municipal corporations and that part of the quasi-municipal corporation known as the county of Arapahoe, in the state of Colorado, included within the exterior boundaries of the said city of Denver as the same shall be bounded when this amendment takes effect, are hereby consolidated and are hereby declared to be a single body politic and corporate, by the name of the "City and County of Denver." By that name said corporation shall have perpetual succession, and shall own, possess, and hold all property, real and personal, theretofore owned, possessed, or held by the said city of Denver and by such included municipal corporations, and also all property, real and personal, theretofore owned, possessed, or held by the said county of Arapahoe, and shall assume, manage, and dispose of all trusts in any way connected therewith; shall succeed to all the rights and liabilities, and shall acquire all benefits and shall assume and pay all bonds, obligations, and indebtedness of said city of Denver and of said included municipal corporations and of the county of Arapahoe; by that name may sue and defend, plead and be impleaded, in all courts and places, and in all matters and proceedings; may have and use a common seal and alter the same at pleasure; may purchase, receive, hold, and enjoy or sell and dispose of, real and personal property; may receive bequests, gifts, and donations of all kinds of property, in fee simple, or in trust for public, charitable, or other purposes; and do all things and acts necessary to carry out the purposes of such gifts, bequests, and donations, with power to manage, sell, lease, or otherwise dispose of the same in accordance with the terms of the gift, bequest, or trust; shall have the power, within or without its territorial limits, to construct, condemn and purchase, purchase, acquire, lease, add to, maintain, conduct, and operate water works, light plants, power plants, transportation systems, heating plants, and any other public utilities or works or ways local in use and extent, in whole or in part, and everything required therefore, for the use of said city and county and the inhabitants

thereof, and any such systems, plants, or works or ways, or any contracts in relation or connection with either, that may exist and which said city and county may desire to purchase, in whole or in part, the same or any part thereof may be purchased by said city and county which may enforce such purchase by proceedings at law as in taking land for public use by right of eminent domain, and shall have the power to issue bonds upon the vote of the taxpaying electors, at any special or general election, in any amount necessary to carry out any of said powers or purposes, as may by the charter be provided.

The provisions of section 3 of article XIV of this constitution and the general annexation and consolidation statutes of the state relating to counties shall apply to the city and county of Denver. Any contiguous town, city, or territory hereafter annexed to or consolidated with the city and county of Denver, under any such laws of this state, in whatsoever county the same may be at the time, shall be detached per se from such other county and become a municipal and territorial part of the city and county of Denver, together with all property thereunto belonging.

The city and county of Denver shall alone always constitute one judicial district of the state.

Any other provisions of this constitution to the contrary notwithstanding:

No annexation or consolidation proceeding shall be initiated after the effective date of this amendment pursuant to the general annexation and consolidation statutes of the state of Colorado to annex lands to or consolidate lands with the city and county of Denver until such proposed annexation or consolidation is first approved by a majority vote of a six-member boundary control commission composed of one commissioner from each of the boards of county commissioners of Adams, Arapahoe, and Jefferson counties, respectively, and three elected officials of the city and county of Denver to be chosen by the mayor. The commissioners from each of the said counties shall be appointed by resolution of their respective boards.

No land located in any county other than Adams, Arapahoe, or Jefferson counties shall be annexed to or consolidated with the city and county of Denver unless such annexation or consolidation is approved by the unanimous vote of all the members of the board of county commissioners of the county in which such land is located.

All actions, including actions regarding procedural rules, shall be adopted by the commission by majority vote. Each commissioner shall have one vote, including the commissioner who acts as the chairman of the commission. All procedural rules adopted by the commission shall be filed with the secretary of state.
This amendment shall be self-executing.

Section 2. Officers
The officers of the city and county of Denver shall be such as by appointment or election may be provided for by the charter; and the jurisdiction, term of office, duties and qualifications of all such officers shall be such as in the charter may be provided; but the charter shall designate the officers who shall, respectively, perform the acts and duties required of county officers to be done by the constitution or by the general law, as far as applicable. If any officer of said city and county of Denver shall receive any compensation whatever, he or she shall receive the same as a stated salary, the amount of which shall be fixed by the charter, or, in the case of officers not in the classified civil service, by ordinance within limits fixed by the charter; provided, however, no elected officer shall receive any increase or decrease in compensation under any ordinance passed during the term for which he was elected.

Section 3. Establishment of Government Civil Service Recommendations
Immediately upon the canvass of the vote showing the adoption of this amendment, it shall be the duty of the governor of the state to issue his proclamation accordingly. Every charter shall provide that the department of fire and police and the department of public utilities and works shall be under such civil service regulations as in said charter shall be provided.

Section 4. First Charter

(1) The people of the city and county of Denver are hereby vested with and they shall always have the exclusive power in making, altering, revising or amending their charter.
(2) and (3) Deleted.
(4) Any franchise relating to any street, alley, or public place of the said city and county shall be subject to the initiative and referendum powers reserved to the people under section 1 of article V of this constitution. Such referendum power shall be guaranteed notwithstanding a recital in an ordinance granting such franchise that such ordinance is necessary for the immediate preservation of the public peace, health, and safety. Not more than five percent of the registered electors of a home rule city shall be required to order such referendum. Nothing in this section shall preclude a home rule charter provision which requires a lesser number of registered electors to order such referendum or which requires a franchise to be voted on by the registered electors. If such a referendum is ordered to be submitted to the registered electors, the grantee of such franchise shall deposit with the treasurer the expense (to be determined by said treasurer) of such submission. The council shall have power to fix the rate of taxation on property each year for city and county purposes.

Section 5. New charters, Amendments or Measures

The citizens of the city and county of Denver shall have the exclusive power to amend their charter or to adopt a new charter, or to adopt any measure as herein provided;
It shall be competent for qualified electors in number not less than five percent of the next preceding gubernatorial vote in said city and county to petition the council for any measure, or charter amendment, or for a charter convention. The council shall submit the same to a vote of the qualified electors at the next general election not held within thirty days after such petition is filed; whenever such petition is signed by qualified electors in number not less than ten percent of the next preceding gubernatorial vote in said city and county, with a

request for a special election, the council shall submit it at a special election to be held not less than thirty nor more than sixty days from the date of filing the petition; provided, that any question so submitted at a special election shall not again be submitted at a special election within two years thereafter. In submitting any such charter, charter amendment or measure, any alternative article or proposition may be presented for the choice of the voters, and may be voted on separately without prejudice to others. Whenever the question of a charter convention is carried by a majority of those voting thereon, a charter convention shall be called through a special election ordinance as provided in section four (4) hereof, and the same shall be constituted and held and the proposed charter submitted to a vote of the qualified electors, approved or rejected, and all expenses paid, as in said section provided.

The clerk of the city and county shall publish, with his official certification, for three times, a week apart, in the official newspapers, the first publication to be with his call for the election, general or special, the full text of any charter, charter amendment, measure, or proposal for a charter convention, or alternative article or proposition, which is to be submitted to the voters. Within ten days following the vote the said clerk shall publish once in said newspaper the full text of any charter, charter amendment, measure, or proposal for a charter convention, or alternative article or proposition, which shall have been approved by majority of those voting thereon, and he shall file with the secretary of state two copies thereof (with the vote for and against) officially certified by him, and the same shall go into effect from the date of such filing. He shall also certify to the secretary of state, with the vote for and against, two copies of every defeated alternative article or proposition, charter, charter amendment, measure or proposal for a charter convention. Each charter shall also provide for a reference upon proper petition therefor, of measures passed by the council to a vote of the qualified electors, and for the initiative by the qualified electors of such ordinances as they may by petition request.

The signatures to petitions in this amendment mentioned need not all be on one paper. Nothing herein or elsewhere shall prevent the council, if it sees fit, from adopting automatic vote registers for use at elections and references.

No charter, charter amendment or measure adopted or defeated under the provisions of this amendment shall be amended, repealed or revived, except by petition and electoral vote. And no such charter, charter amendment or measure shall diminish the tax rate for state purposes fixed by act of the general assembly, or interfere in any wise with the collection of state taxes.

The city council, or board of trustees, or other body in which the legislative powers of any home rule city or town may then be vested, on its own initiative, may submit any measure, charter amendment, or the question whether or not a charter convention shall be called, at any general or special state or municipal election held not less than 30 days after the effective date of the ordinance or resolution submitting such question to the voters.

Section 6. **Home Rule for Cities and Towns**

The people of each city or town of this state, having a population of two thousand inhabitants as determined by the last preceding census taken under the authority of the United States, the state of Colorado or said city or town, are hereby vested with, and they shall always have, power to make, amend, add to or replace the charter of said city or town, which shall be its organic law and extend to all its local and municipal matters.

Such charter and the ordinances made pursuant thereto in such matters shall supersede within the territorial limits and other jurisdiction of said city or town any law of the state in conflict therewith.

Proposals for charter conventions shall be submitted by the city council or board of trustees, or other body in which the legislative powers of the city or town shall then be vested, at special elections, or at general, state or municipal elections, upon petition filed by qualified electors, all in reasonable conformity with section 5 of this article, and all proceedings thereon or thereafter shall be in reasonable conformity with sections 4 and 5 of this article.

From and after the certifying to and filing with the secretary of state of a charter framed and approved in reasonable conformity with the provisions of this article, such city or town, and the citizens thereof, shall have the powers set out in sections 1, 4 and 5 of this article, and all other powers necessary, requisite or proper for the government and administration of its local and municipal matters, including power to legislate upon, provide, regulate, conduct and control:

a. The creation and terms of municipal officers, agencies and employments; the definition, regulation and alteration of the powers, duties, qualifications and terms or tenure of all municipal officers, agents and employees;
b. The creation of police courts; the definition and regulation of the jurisdiction, powers and duties thereof, and the election or appointment of police magistrates therefor;
c. The creation of municipal courts; the definition and regulation of the jurisdiction, powers and duties thereof, and the election or appointment of the officers thereof;
d. All matters pertaining to municipal elections in such city or town, and to electoral votes therein on measures submitted under the charter or ordinances thereof, including the calling or notice and the date of such election or vote, the registration of voters, nominations, nomination and election systems, judges and clerks of election, the form of ballots, balloting, challenging, canvassing, certifying the result, securing the purity of elections, guarding against abuses of the elective franchise, and tending to make such elections or electoral votes nonpartisan in character;
e. The issuance, refunding and liquidation of all kinds of municipal obligations, including bonds and other obligations of park, water and local improvement districts;
f. The consolidation and management of park or water districts in such cities or towns or within the jurisdiction thereof; but no such consolidation shall be effective until approved by the vote of a majority, in each district to be consolidated, of the qualified electors voting therein upon the question;
g. The assessment of property in such city or town for municipal taxation and the levy and collection of taxes thereon for

municipal purposes and special assessments for local improvements; such assessments, levy and collection of taxes and special assessments to be made by municipal officials or by the county or state officials as may be provided by the charter;
h. The imposition, enforcement and collection of fines and penalties for the violation of any of the provisions of the charter, or of any ordinance adopted in pursuance of the charter.

It is the intention of this article to grant and confirm to the people of all municipalities coming within its provisions the full right of self-government in both local and municipal matters and the enumeration herein of certain powers shall not be construed to deny such cities and towns, and to the people thereof, any right or power essential or proper to the full exercise of such right.

The statutes of the state of Colorado, so faras applicable, shall continue to apply to such cities and towns, except insofar as superseded by the charters of such cities and towns or by ordinance passed pursuant to such charters.

All provisions of the charters of the city and county of Denver and the cities of Pueblo, Colorado Springs and Grand Junction, as heretofore certified to and filed with the secretary of state, and of the charter of any other city heretofore approved by a majority of those voting thereon and certified to and filed with the secretary of state, which provisions are not in conflict with this article, and all elections and electoral votes heretofore had under and pursuant thereto, are hereby ratified, affirmed and validated as of their date.

Any act in violation of the provisions of such charter or of any ordinance thereunder shall be criminal and punishable as such when so provided by any statute now or hereafter in force.

The provisions of this section 6 shall apply to the city and county of Denver.

This article shall be in all respects self-executing.

Section 7. City and County of Denver Single School District -Consolidations

The city and county of Denver shall alone always constitute one school district, to be known as District No. 1, but its conduct, affairs and business shall be in the hands of a board of education consisting of such numbers, elected in such manner as the general school laws of the state shall provide.

The said board of education shall perform all the acts and duties required to be performed for said district by the general laws of the state. Except as inconsistent with this amendment, the general school laws of the state shall, unless the context evinces a contrary intent, be held to extend and apply to the said "District No. 1".

Upon the annexation of any contiguous municipality which shall include a school district or districts or any part of a district, said school district or districts or part shall be merged in said "District No. 1", which shall then own all the property thereof, real and personal, located within the boundaries of such annexed municipality, and shall assume and pay all the bonds, obligations and indebtedness of each of the said included school districts, and a proper proportion of those of partially included districts. Provided, however, that the indebtedness, both principal and interest, which any school district may be under at the time when it becomes a part, by this amendment or by annexation, of said "District No. 1", shall be paid by said school district so owing the same by a special tax to be fixed and certified by the board of education to the council which shall levy the same upon the property within the boundaries of such district, respectively, as the same existed at the time such district becomes a part of said "District No. 1", and in case of partially included districts such tax shall be equitably apportioned upon the several parts thereof.

Section 8. Conflicting Constitutional Provisions Declared Inapplicable

Anything in the constitution of this state in conflict or inconsistent with the provisions of this amendment is hereby declared to be inapplicable to the matters and things by this amendment covered and provided for.

Section 9. Procedure and Requirements for Adoption

(1) Notwithstanding any provision in sections 4, 5, and 6 of this article to the contrary, the registered electors of each city and county, city, and town of the state are hereby vested with the power to adopt, amend, and repeal a home rule charter.
(2) The general assembly shall provide by statute procedures under which the registered electors of any proposed or existing city and county, city, or town may adopt, amend, and repeal a municipal home rule charter. Action to initiate home rule shall be by petition, signed by not less than five percent of the registered electors of the proposed or existing city and county, city, or town, or by proper ordinance by the city council or board of trustees of a town, submitting the question of the adoption of a municipal home rule charter to the registered electors of the city and county, city, or town. No municipal home rule charter, amendment thereto, or repeal thereof, shall become effective until approved by a majority of the registered electors of such city and county, city, or town voting thereon. A new city or town may acquire home rule status at the time of its incorporation.
(3) The provisions of this article as they existed prior to the effective date of this section, as they relate to procedures for the initial adoption of home rule charters and for the amendment of existing home rule charters, shall continue to apply until superseded by statute.
(4) It is the purpose of this section to afford to the people of all cities, cities and counties, and towns the right to home rule regardless of population, period of incorporation, or other limitation, and for this purpose this section shall be self-executing. It is the further purpose of this section to facilitate adoption and amendment of home rule through such procedures

as may hereafter be enacted by the general assembly.

Section 10. City and County of Broomfield - Created
The city of Broomfield is a preexisting municipal corporation and home rule city of the state of Colorado, physically situated in parts of Adams, Boulder, Jefferson, and Weld counties. On and after November 15, 2001, all territory in the municipal boundaries of the city of Broomfield shall be detached from the counties of Adams, Boulder, Jefferson, and Weld and shall be consolidated into a single county and municipal corporation with the name "The City and County of Broomfield." Prior to November 15, 2001, the city of Broomfield shall not extend its boundaries beyond the annexation boundary map approved by the Broomfield city council on April 28, 1998, as an amendment to the city of Broomfield 1995 master plan. The existing charter of the said city of Broomfield shall become the charter of the city and county of Broomfield.

The city and county of Broomfield shall have perpetual succession; shall own, possess, and hold all real and personal property, including water rights, the right to use water, and contracts for water, currently owned, possessed, or held by the said city of Broomfield; shall assume, manage, and dispose of all trusts in any way connected therewith; shall succeed to all the rights and liabilities of, shall acquire all benefits of, and shall assume and pay all bonds, obligations, and indebtedness of said city of Broomfield and its proportionate share of the general obligation indebtedness and, as provided by intergovernmental agreement, its proportionate share of revenue bond obligations of the counties of Adams, Boulder, Jefferson, and Weld on and after November 15, 2001.

The city and county of Broomfield may sue and defend, plead, and be impleaded in all courts and in all matters and proceedings; may have and use a common seal and alter the same at pleasure; may grant franchises; may purchase, receive, hold, and enjoy, or sell and dispose of real and personal property; may receive bequests, gifts, and donations of real and personal property, or real and personal property in trust for public, charitable, or other purposes, and do all things and acts necessary to carry out the purposes of such gifts, bequests, donations, and trusts with power to manage, sell, lease, or otherwise dispose of the same in accordance with the terms of the gift, bequest, donation, or trust.

The city and county of Broomfield shall have the power within and without its territorial limits to construct, condemn, purchase, acquire, lease, add to, maintain, conduct, and operate water works, water supplies, sanitary sewer facilities, storm water facilities, parks, recreation facilities, open space lands, light plants, power plants, heating plants, electric and other energy facilities and systems, gas facilities and systems, transportation systems, cable television systems, telecommunication systems, and other public utilities or works or ways local in use and extent, in whole or in part, and everything required therefor, for the use of said city and county and the inhabitants thereof; to purchase in whole or in part any such systems, plants, works, facilities, or ways, or any contracts in relation or connection thereto that may exist, and may enforce such purchase by proceedings at law as in taking land for public use by right of eminent domain; and to issue bonds in accordance with its charter in any amount necessary to carry out any said powers or purposes, as the charter may provide and limit. The city and county of Broomfield shall have all of the powers of its charter and shall have all of the powers set out in section 6 of this article, including the power to make, amend, add to, or replace its charter as set forth in section 9 of this article. The charter provisions and procedures shall supersede any constitutional or statutory limitations and procedures regarding financial obligations. The city and county of Broomfield shall have all powers conferred to home rule municipalities and to home rule counties by the constitution and general laws of the state of Colorado that are not inconsistent with the constitutional provisions creating the city and county of Broomfield.

Prior to November 15, 2001, the charter and ordinances of the city of Broomfield shall govern all local and municipal matters of the city. On and after November 15, 2001, the constitutional provisions creating and governing the city and county of Broomfield, the city and county charter adopted in accordance with these constitutional provisions, and the ordinances existing and adopted from time to time shall govern all local and municipal matters of the city and county of Broomfield.

On and after November 15, 2001, the requirements of section 3 of article XIV of this constitution and the general annexation and consolidation statutes of the state relating to counties shall apply to the city and county of Broomfield. On and after November 15, 2001, any contiguous territory, together with all property belonging thereto, hereafter annexed to or consolidated with the city and county of Broomfield under any laws of this state, in whatsoever county the same may be at the time, shall be detached from such other county and become a municipal and territorial part of the city and county of Broomfield.

On and after November 15, 2001, no annexation or consolidation proceeding shall be initiated pursuant to the general annexation and consolidation statutes of the state to annex lands to or consolidate lands with the city and county of Broomfield until such proposed annexation or consolidation is first approved by a majority vote of a seven-member boundary control commission. The boundary control commission shall be composed of one commissioner from each of the boards of commissioners of Adams, Boulder, Jefferson, and Weld counties, respectively, and three elected officials of the city and county of Broomfield. The commissioners from each of the said counties shall be appointed by resolution of the respective county boards of commissioners. The three elected officials from the city and county of Broomfield shall be appointed by the mayor of the city and county of Broomfield. The boundary control commission shall adopt all actions, including actions regarding procedural rules, by majority vote. Each member of the boundary control commission shall have one vote, including the commissioner who acts as chairperson of the commission. The commission shall file all procedural rules adopted by the commission with the secretary of state.

Enacted by the people November 3, 1998 -- Effective upon proclamation of the Governor, January --, 1999. (For the text of this amendment and the votes cast thereon, see L. 98, p. 2225.)

Section 11. Officers - City and County of Broomfield
The officers of the city and county of Broomfield shall be as provided for by its charter or ordinances. The jurisdiction, term of office, and duties of such officers shall commence on November 15, 2001. The qualifications and duties of all such officers shall be as provided for by the city and county charter and ordinances, but the ordinances shall designate the officers who shall perform the acts and duties required of county officers pursuant to this constitution or the general laws of the state of Colorado, as far as applicable. All compensation for elected officials shall be determined by ordinance and not by state statute. If any elected officer of the city and county of Broomfield shall receive any compensation, such officer shall receive the same as a stated salary, the amount of which shall be fixed by ordinance within limits fixed by the city and county charter or by resolution approving the city and county budget and paid in equal monthly payments. No elected officer shall receive any increase or decrease in compensation under any ordinance or resolution passed during the term for which such officer was elected.

Section 12. Transfer of Government
Upon the canvass of the vote showing the adoption of the constitutional provisions creating and governing the city and county of Broomfield, the governor shall issue a proclamation accordingly, and, on and after November 15, 2001, the city of Broomfield and those parts of the counties of Adams, Boulder, Jefferson, and Weld included in the boundaries of said city shall be consolidated into the city and county of Broomfield. The duties and terms of office of all officers of Adams, Boulder, Jefferson, and Weld counties shall no longer be applicable to and shall terminate with regard to the city and county of Broomfield.

On and after November 15, 2001, the terms of office of the mayor and city council of the city of Broomfield shall terminate with regard to the city of Broomfield and said mayor and city council shall become the mayor and city council of the city and county of Broomfield. The city council of the city and county of Broomfield, in addition to performing the duties prescribed in the city and county charter and ordinances, shall perform the duties of a board of county commissioners or may delegate certain duties to various boards and commissions appointed by the city council of the city and county of Broomfield. The city and county of Broomfield shall be a successor district of the city of Broomfield under section 20 of article X of this constitution. Any voter approval granted the city of Broomfield under section 20 of article X of this constitution prior to November 15, 2001, shall be considered voter approval under said section for the city and county of Broomfield. The city and county of Broomfield shall have the power to continue to impose and collect sales, use, and property taxes that were imposed by the city of Broomfield and the counties of Adams, Boulder, Jefferson, and Weld within the areas where said taxes were imposed on November 14, 2001, until the voters of the city and county of Broomfield approve uniform sales, use, and property taxes within the city and county of Broomfield or approve increased sales, use, or property taxes within the city and county of Broomfield. Any violation of any criminal statutes of the state of Colorado occurring on or before November 14, 2001, shall continue to be prosecuted within the county where the violation originally occurred.

Section 13 Sections Self-executing - Appropriations
Sections 10 through 13 of this article shall be in all respects self-executing and shall be construed so as to supersede any conflicting constitutional or statutory provision that would otherwise impede the creation of the city and county of Broomfield or limit any of the provisions of those sections. Except as otherwise provided in sections 10 through 13, said sections shall be effective on and after November 15, 2001. After the adoption of the constitutional provisions creating and governing the city and county of Broomfield, the general assembly may

appropriate funds, if necessary, in cooperation with the city and county of Broomfield to implement these constitutional provisions at the state level.

Article XXI: Recall from Office

Section 1. State Officers May Be Recalled.
Every elective public officer of the state of Colorado may be recalled from office at any time by the registered electors entitled to vote for a successor of such incumbent through the procedure and in the manner herein provided for, which procedure shall be known as the recall, and shall be in addition to and without excluding any other method of removal provided by law.
The procedure hereunder to effect the recall of an elective public officer shall be as follows:

A petition signed by registered electors entitled to vote for a successor of the incumbent sought to be recalled, equal in number to twenty-five percent of the entire vote cast at the last preceding election for all candidates for the position which the incumbent sought to be recalled occupies, demanding an election of the successor to the officer named in said petition, shall be filed in the office in which petitions for nominations to office held by the incumbent sought to be recalled are required to be filed; provided, if more than one person is required by law to be elected to fill the office of which the person sought to be recalled is an incumbent, then the said petition shall be signed by registered electors entitled to vote for a successor to the incumbent sought to be recalled equal in number to twenty-five percent of the entire vote cast at the last preceding general election for all candidates for the office, to which the incumbent sought to be recalled was elected as one of the officers thereof, said entire vote being divided by the number of all officers elected to such office, at the last preceding general election; and such petition shall contain a general statement, in not more than two hundred words, of the ground or grounds on which such recall is sought, which statement is intended for the information of the registered electors, and the registered electors shall be the sole and exclusive judges of the legality, reasonableness and sufficiency of such ground or grounds assigned for such recall, and said ground or grounds shall not be open to review.

Section 2. Form of Recall Petition.
Any recall petition may be circulated and signed in sections, provided each section shall contain a full and accurate copy of the title and text of the petition; and such recall petition shall be filed in the office in which petitions for nominations to office held by the incumbent sought to be recalled are required to be filed. The signatures to such recall petition need not all be on one sheet of paper, but each signer must add to his signature the date of his signing said petition, and his place of residence, giving his street number, if any, should he reside in a town or city. The person circulating such sheet must make and subscribe an oath on said sheet that the signatures thereon are genuine, and a false oath, willfully so made and subscribed by such person, shall be perjury and be punished as such. All petitions shall be deemed and held to be sufficient if they appear to be signed by the requisite number of signers, and such signers shall be deemed and held to be registered electors, unless a protest in writing under oath shall be filed in the office in which such petition has been filed, by some registered elector, within fifteen days after such petition is filed, setting forth specifically the grounds of such protest, whereupon the officer with whom such petition is filed shall forthwith mail a copy of such protest to the person or persons named in such petition as representing the signers thereof, together with a notice fixing a time for hearing such protest not less than five nor more than ten days after such notice is mailed. All hearings shall be before the officer with whom such protest is filed, and all testimony shall be under oath. Such hearings shall be summary and not subject to delay, and must be concluded within thirty days after such petition is filed, and the result thereof shall be forthwith certified to the person or persons representing the signers of such petition. In case the petition is not sufficient it may be withdrawn by the person or a majority of the persons representing the signers of such petition, and may, within fifteen days thereafter, be amended and refiled as an original petition. The finding as to the sufficiency of any petition may be reviewed by any state court of general jurisdiction in the county in which such petition is filed, upon application of the person or a majority of the persons

representing the signers of such petition, but such review shall be had and determined forthwith. The sufficiency, or the determination of the sufficiency, of the petition referred to in this section shall not be held, or construed, to refer to the ground or grounds assigned in such petition for the recall of the incumbent sought to be recalled from office thereby.

When such petition is sufficient, the officer with whom such recall petition was filed, shall forthwith submit said petition, together with a certificate of its sufficiency to the governor, who shall thereupon order and fix the date for holding the election not less than thirty days nor more than sixty days from the date of submission of said petition; provided, if a general election is to be held within ninety days after the date of submission of said petition, the recall election shall be held as part of said general election.

Section 3. Resignation Filling Vacancy.
If such officer shall offer his resignation, it shall be accepted, and the vacancy caused by such resignation, or from any other cause, shall be filled as provided by law; but the person appointed to fill such vacancy shall hold his office only until the person elected at the recall election shall qualify. If such officer shall not resign within five days after the sufficiency of the recall petition shall have been sustained, the governor shall make or cause to be made publication of notice for the holding of such election, and officers charged by law with duties concerning elections shall make all arrangements for such election, and the same shall be conducted, returned and the result thereof declared in all respects as in the case of general elections.

On the official ballot at such elections shall be printed in not more than 200 words, the reasons set forth in the petition for demanding his recall, and in not more than three hundred words there shall also be printed, if desired by him, the officer's justification of his course in office. If such officer shall resign at any time subsequent to the filing thereof, the recall election shall be called notwithstanding such resignation.

There shall be printed on the official ballot, as to every officer whose recall is to be voted on, the words, "Shall (name of person against whom the recall petition is filed) be recalled from the office of (title of the office)?" Following such question shall be the words, "Yes" and "No", on separate lines, with a blank space at the right of each, in which the voter shall indicate, by marking a cross (X), his vote for or against such recall.

On such ballots, under each question, there shall also be printed the names of those persons who have been nominated as candidates to succeed the person sought to be recalled; but no vote cast shall be counted for any candidate for such office, unless the voter also voted for or against the recall of such person sought to be recalled from said office. The name of the person against whom the petition is filed shall not appear on the ballot as a candidate for the office.

If a majority of those voting on said question of the recall of any incumbent from office shall vote "no", said incumbent shall continue in said office; if a majority shall vote "yes", such incumbent shall thereupon be deemed removed from such office upon the qualification of his successor.

If the vote had in such recall elections shall recall the officer then the candidate who has received the highest number of votes for the office thereby vacated shall be declared elected for the remainder of the term, and a certificate of election shall be forthwith issued to him by the canvassing board. In case the person who received the highest number of votes shall fail to qualify within fifteen days after the issuance of a certificate of election, the office shall be deemed vacant, and shall be filled according to law.

Candidates for the office may be nominated by petition, as now provided by law, which petition shall be filed in the office in which petitions for nomination to office are required by law to be filed not less than fifteen days before such recall election.

Section 4. Limitation Municipal Corporations May Adopt, When.

No recall petition shall be circulated or filed against any officer until he has actually held his office for at least six months, save and except it may be filed against any member of the state legislature at any time after five days from the convening and organizing of the legislature after his election.

After one recall petition and election, no further petition shall be filed against the same officer during the term for which he was elected, unless the petitioners signing said petition shall equal fifty percent of the votes cast at the last preceding general election for all of the candidates for the office held by such officer as herein above defined.

In any recall election of a state elective officer, if the incumbent whose recall is sought is not recalled, he shall be repaid from the state treasury for the expenses of such election in the manner provided by law. The general assembly may establish procedures for the reimbursement by a local governmental entity of expenses incurred by an incumbent elective officer of such governmental entity whose recall is sought but who is not recalled.

If the governor is sought to be recalled under the provisions of this article, the duties herein imposed upon him shall be performed by the lieutenant-governor; and if the secretary of state is sought to be recalled, the duties herein imposed upon him, shall be performed by the state auditor.

The recall may also be exercised by the registered electors of each county, city and county, city and town of the state, with reference to the elective officers thereof, under such procedure as shall be provided by law.

Until otherwise provided by law, the legislative body of any such county, city and county, city and town may provide for the manner of exercising such recall powers in such counties, cities and counties, cities and towns, but shall not require any such recall to be signed by registered electors more in number than twenty-five percent of the entire vote cast at the last preceding election, as in section 1 hereof more particularly set forth, for all the candidates for office which the incumbent sought to be recalled occupies, as herein above defined.

Every person having authority to exercise or exercising any public or governmental duty, power or function, shall be an elective officer, or one appointed, drawn or designated in accordance with law by an elective officer or officers, or by some board, commission, person or persons legally appointed by an elective officer or officers, each of which said elective officers shall be subject to the recall provision of this constitution; provided, that, subject to regulation by law, any person may, without compensation therefor, file petitions, or complaints in courts concerning crimes, or do police duty only in cases of immediate danger to person or property.

Nothing herein contained shall be construed as affecting or limiting the present or future powers of cities and counties or cities having charters adopted under the authority given by the constitution, except as in the last three preceding paragraphs expressed.

In the submission to the electors of any petition proposed under this article, all officers shall be guided by the general laws of the state, except as otherwise herein provided.

This article is self-executing, but legislation may be enacted to facilitate its operations, but in no way limiting or restricting the provisions of this article, or the powers herein reserved.

Article XXII: Intoxicating Liquors

Section 1. Repeal of Intoxicating Liquor Laws.

Repealed.

Article XXIII: Publication of Legal Advertising

Repealed.

Article XXIV: Old Age Pensions

Section 1. Fund Created.
A fund to be known as the old age pension fund is hereby created and established in the treasury of the state of Colorado.

Section 2. Moneys Allocated to Fund.
There is hereby set aside, allocated and allotted to the old age pension fund sums and money as follows:

(a) Eighty-five percent of all net revenue accrued or accruing, received or receivable from any and all excise taxes now or hereafter levied upon sales at retail, or any other purchase transaction; together with eighty-five percent of the net revenue derived from any excise taxes now or hereafter levied upon the storage, use, or consumption of any commodity or product; together with eighty-five percent of all license fees imposed by article 26 of title 39, Colorado Revised Statutes, and amendments thereto; provided, however, that no part of the revenue derived from excise taxes now or hereafter levied, for highway purposes, upon gasoline or other motor fuel, shall be made a part of said old age pension fund.
(b) Eighty-five percent of all net revenue accrued or accruing, received or receivable from taxes of whatever kind upon all malt, vinous, or spirituous liquor, both intoxicating and non-intoxicating, and license fees connected therewith.
(c) Deleted
(d) All grants in aid from the federal government for old age assistance.
(e) Deleted.
(f) Such other money as may be allocated to said fund by the general assembly.

Section 3. Persons Entitled to Receive Pensions.
Every citizen of the United States who has been a resident of the state of Colorado for such period as the general assembly may determine, who has attained the age of sixty years or more, and who qualifies under the laws of Colorado to receive a pension,

shall be entitled to receive the same; provided, however, that no person otherwise qualified shall be denied a pension by reason of the fact that the person is the owner of real estate occupied by the person as a residence; nor for the reason that relatives may be financially able to contribute to the person's support and maintenance; nor shall any person be denied a pension for the reason that the person owns personal property which by law is exempt from execution or attachment; nor shall any person be required, in order to receive a pension, to repay, or promise to repay, the state of Colorado any money paid to the person as an old age pension.

Section 4. The State Board of Public Welfare to Administer Fund.

The state board of public welfare, or such other agency as may be authorized by law to administer old age pensions, shall cause all moneys deposited in the old age pension fund to be paid out as directed by this article and as required by statutory provisions not inconsistent with the provisions hereof, after defraying the expense of administering the said fund.

Section 5. Revenues for Old Age Pension Fund Continued.

The excise tax on sales at retail, together with all license fees levied by article 26 of title 39, Colorado Revised Statutes, and amendments thereto, are hereby continued in full force and effect beyond the date on which said taxes and license fees would otherwise expire, and shall continue until repealed or amended; provided, however, that no law providing revenue for the old age pension fund shall be repealed, nor shall any such law be amended so as to reduce the revenue provided for the old age pension fund, except in the event that at the time of such repeal or amendment, revenue is provided for the old age pension fund in an amount at least equal to that provided by the measure amended or repealed during the calendar year immediately preceding the proposed amendment or repeal.

Section 6. Basic Minimum Award.

(a) Beginning on the effective date of this article, every person entitled to and receiving an old age pension from the state of Colorado under any former law or constitutional provision shall be entitled to receive the basic minimum award hereinafter provided for, without being required to make a new application therefor, and such basic minimum award shall be paid each month thereafter, so long as he remains qualified, to each person receiving an old age pension at the time of the adoption of this article, and such basic minimum award shall likewise be paid to each person who hereafter becomes qualified to receive an old age pension; subject, however, to the provisions of this article relating to net income from other sources.
(b) From and after the effective date of this article, the basic minimum award payable to those persons qualified to receive an old age pension shall be one hundred dollars monthly, provided, however, that the amount of net income, from whatever source, that any person qualified to receive a pension may have shall be deducted from the amount of the pension award unless otherwise provided by law.
(c) The state board of public welfare, or such other agency as may be authorized by law to administer old age pensions, shall have the power to adjust the basic minimum award above one hundred dollars per month if, in its discretion, living costs have changed sufficiently to justify that action.

Section 7. Stabilization Fund and Health and Medical Care Fund.

(a) All the moneys deposited in the old age pension fund shall be first available for payment of basic minimum awards to qualified recipients, and no part of said fund shall be transferred to any other fund until such basic minimum awards shall have been paid.

(b) Any moneys remaining in the old age pension fund after full payment of such basic minimum awards shall be transferred to a fund to be known as the stabilization fund, which fund shall be maintained at the amount of five million dollars, and restored to that amount after any disbursements therefrom. The state board of public welfare, or such other agency as may be authorized by law to administer old age pensions, shall use the moneys in such fund only to stabilize payments of basic minimum awards.

(c) Any moneys remaining in the old age pension fund, after full payment of basic minimum awards and after establishment and maintenance of the stabilization fund in the amount of five million dollars, shall be transferred to a healthand medical care fund. The state board of public welfare, or such other agency as may be authorized by law to administer old age pensions, shall establish and promulgate rules and regulations for administration of a program to provide health and medical care to persons who qualify to receive old age pensions and who are not patients in an institution for tuberculosis or mental disease; the costs of such program, not to exceed ten million dollars in any fiscal year, shall be defrayed from such health and medical care fund; provided, however, all moneys available, accrued or accruing, received or receivable, in said health and medical care fund, in excess of ten million dollars in any fiscal year shall be transferred to the general fund of the state to be used pursuant to law.

Section 8. Fund to Remain Inviolate.

All moneys deposited in the old age pension fund shall remain inviolate for the purpose for which created, and no part thereof shall be transferred to any other fund, or used or appropriated for any other purpose, except as provided for in this article.

Section 9. Effective Date.

Repealed.

Article XXV: Public Utilities

Public Utilities

In addition to the powers now vested in the General Assembly of the State of Colorado, all power to regulate the facilities, service and rates and charges therefore, including facilities and service and rates and charges therefore within home rule cities and home rule towns, of every corporation, individual, or association of individuals, wheresoever situate or operating within the State of Colorado, whether within or without a home rule city or home rule town, as a public utility, as presently or as may hereafter be defined as a public utility by the laws of the State of Colorado, is hereby vested in such agency of the State of Colorado as the General Assembly shall by law designate.

Until such time as the General Assembly may otherwise designate, said authority shall be vested in the Public Utilities Commission of the State of Colorado; provided however, nothing herein shall affect the power of municipalities to exercise reasonable police and licensing powers, nor their power to grant franchises; and provided, further, that nothing herein shall be construed to apply to municipally owned utilities.

Article XXVI: Nuclear Detonations

Section 1. Nuclear Detonations Prohibited -Exceptions
No nuclear explosive device may be detonated or placed in the ground for the purpose of detonation in this state except in accordance with this article.

Section 2. Election Required
Before the emplacement of any nuclear explosive device in the ground in this state, the detonation of that device shall first have been approved by the voters through enactment of an initiated or referred measure authorizing that detonation, such measure having been ordered, proposed, submitted to the voters, and approved as provided in section 1 of article V of this constitution.

Section 3. Certification of Indemnification Required
Before the detonation or emplacement for the purpose of detonation of any nuclear explosive device, a competent state official or agency designated by the governor shall first have certified that sufficient and secure financial resources exist in the form of applicable insurance, self-insurance, indemnity bonds, indemnification agreements, or otherwise, without utilizing state funds, to compensate in full all parties that might foreseeably suffer damage to person or property from ground motion, ionizing radiation, other pollution, or other hazard attributable to such detonation. Damage is attributable to such detonation without regard to negligence and without regard to any concurrent or intervening cause.

Section 4. Article Self--executing
This article shall be in all respects self- executing; but, the general assembly may by law provide for its more effective enforcement and may by law also impose additional restrictions or conditions upon the emplacement or detonation of any nuclear explosive device.

Section 5. Severability
If any provision of this article, or its application in any particular case, is held invalid, the remainder of the article and its application in all other cases shall remain unimpaired.

Article XXVII: Great Outdoors Colorado

Section 1. Great Outdoors Colorado Program.

(1) The people of the State of Colorado intend that the net proceeds of every state-supervised lottery game operated under the authority of Article XVIII, Section 2 shall be guaranteed and permanently dedicated to the preservation, protection, enhancement and management of the state's wildlife, park, river, trail and open space heritage, except as specifically provided in this article. Accordingly, there shall be established the Great Outdoors Colorado Program to preserve, protect, enhance and manage the state's wildlife, park, river, trail and open space heritage. The Great Outdoors Colorado Program shall include:

(a) Wildlife program grants which:

(I) Develop wildlife watching opportunities;
(II) Implement educational programs about wildlife and wildlife environment;
(III) Provide appropriate programs for maintaining Colorado's diverse wildlife heritage;
(IV) Protect crucial wildlife habitats through the acquisition of lands, leases or easements and restore critical areas;
(b) Outdoor recreation program grants which:
(I) Establish and improve state parks and recreation areas throughout the State of Colorado;
(II) Develop appropriate public information and environmental education resources on Colorado's natural resources at state parks, recreation areas, and other locations throughout the state;
(III) Acquire, construct and maintain trails and river greenways;
(IV) Provide water for recreational purposes through the acquisition of water rights or through agreements with holders of water rights, all in accord with applicable state water law;

(c) A program to identify, acquire and manage unique open space and natural areas of statewide significance through grants to the Colorado Divisions of Parks and Outdoor Recreation and Wildlife, or municipalities, counties, or other political subdivision of the State, or nonprofit land conservation organizations, and which will encourage cooperative investments by other public or private entities for these purposes; and
(d) A program for grants to match local investments to acquire, develop and manage open space, parks, and environmental education facilities, and which will encourage cooperative investments by other public or private entities for these purposes.

Section 2. Trust Fund Created.
A fund to be known as the Great Outdoors Colorado Trust Fund, referred to in this article as the "Trust Fund," is hereby created and established in the Treasury of the State of Colorado.

Section 3. Moneys Allocated to Trust Fund.

(1) Beginning with the proceeds from the fourth quarter of the State's Fiscal Year 1992-1993, all proceeds from all programs, including Lotto and every other state-supervised lottery game operated under the authority of Article XVIII, Section 2 of the Colorado Constitution, whether by the Colorado Lottery Commission or otherwise (such programs defined hereafter in this Article as "Lottery Programs"), net of prizes and expenses of the state lottery division and after a sufficient amount of money has been reserved, as of the end of any fiscal quarter, to ensure the operation of the lottery for the ensuing fiscal quarter (such netted proceeds defined hereafter in this Article as "Net Proceeds") are set aside, allocated, allotted, and continuously appropriated as follows, and the Treasurer shall distribute such proceeds no less frequently than quarterly, as follows:

(a) Repealed.

(b) For each quarter including and after the first quarter of the State's Fiscal Year 1998-1999:

(I) Forty percent to the Conservation Trust Fund for distribution to municipalities and counties and other eligible entities for parks, recreation and open space purposes;
(II) Ten percent to the Division of Parks and Outdoor Recreation for the acquisition, development and improvement of new and existing state parks, recreation areas and recreational trails; and
(III) All remaining Net Proceeds in trust to the Board of the Trust Fund, provided, however, that in any state fiscal year in which the portion of the Net Proceeds which would otherwise be given in trust to the State Board of the Trust Fund exceeds the amount of $35 million, to be adjusted each year for changes from the 1992 Consumer Price Index-Denver, the Net Proceeds in excess of such amount or adjusted amount shall be allocated to the General Fund of the State of Colorado.

(c) to (e) Repealed.

(2) From July 1, 1993, the following sums of money and property, in addition to Net Proceeds as set forth in Section 3(1) above, are set aside, allocated, allotted, and continuously appropriated in trust to the Board of the Trust Fund:

(a) All interest derived from moneys held in the Trust Fund;
(b) Any property donated specifically to the State of Colorado for the specific purpose of benefitting the Trust Fund, including contributions, grants, gifts, bequests, donations, and federal, state, or local grants; and
(c) Such other moneys as may be allocated to the Trust Fund by the General Assembly.

Section 4. Fund to Remain Inviolate.
All moneys deposited in the Trust Fund shall remain in trust for the purposes set forth in this article, and no part thereof shall be used or appropriated for any other purpose, nor made subject to any other tax, charge, fee or restriction.

Section 5. Trust Fund Expenditures.
(1)(a) Expenditures from the Trust Fund shall be made in furtherance of the Great Outdoors Colorado Program, and shall commence in State Fiscal Year 1993- 94. The Board of the Trust Fund shall have the duty to assure that expenditures are made for the purposes set forth in this section and in section 6, and that the amounts expended for each of the following purposes over a period of years be substantially equal:

(I) Investments in the wildlife resources of Colorado through the Colorado Division of Wildlife, including the protection and restoration of crucial wildlife habitats, appropriate programs for maintaining Colorado's diverse wildlife heritage, wildlife watching, and educational programs about wildlife and wildlife environment, consistent with the purposes set forth in Section 1 (1) (a) of this article;
(II) Investments in the outdoor recreation resources of Colorado through the Colorado Division of Parks and Outdoor Recreation, including the State Parks System, trails, public information and environmental education resources, and water for recreational facilities, consistent with the purposes set forth in Section 1 (1) (b) of this article;
(III) Competitive grants to the Colorado Divisions of Parks and Outdoor Recreation and Wildlife, and to counties, municipalities or other political subdivisions of the state, or nonprofit land conservation organizations, to identify, acquire and manage open space and natural areas of statewide significance, consistent with the purposes set forth in Section 1 (1) (c) of this article; and
(IV) Competitive matching grants to local governments or other entities which are eligible for distributions from the conservation trust fund, to acquire, develop or manage open lands and parks, consistent with the purposes set forth in Section 1 (1) (d) of this article;

(b) Provided, however, that the State Board of the Great Outdoors Colorado Trust Fund shall have the discretion (a) to direct that any portion of available revenues be reinvested in the Trust Fund and not expended in any particular year, (b) to make other expenditures which it considers necessary.

Section 6. The State Board of the Great Outdoors Colorado Trust Fund.

(1) There shall be established a State Board of the Great Outdoors Colorado Trust Fund. The Board shall consist of two members of the public from each congressional district, a representative designated by the State Board of Parks and Outdoor Recreation, a representative designated by the Colorado Wildlife Commission, and the Executive Director of the Department of Natural Resources. The public members of the Board shall be appointed by the Governor, subject to the consent of the Senate, for terms of four years--provided, however, that when the first such members are appointed, one of the public members from each congressional district shall be appointed for a two-year term, to assure staggered terms of office thereafter. At least two members shall reside west of the Continental Divide. At least one member shall represent agricultural interests. The public members of the board shall be entitled to a reasonable per diem compensation to be determined by the Board plus their actual expenses for each meeting of the Board or a committee of the Board. The Board's composition shall reflect, to the extent practical, Colorado's gender, ethnic and racial diversity, and no two of the representatives of any one congressional district shall be members of the same political party. Members of the Board shall be subject to removal as provided in Article IV, Section 6 of this constitution.

(2) The Board shall be responsible for, and shall have the power to undertake the following actions:

(a) To direct the Treasurer to disburse expendable income from the Trust Fund as the Board may determine by resolution, and otherwise to administer the Trust Fund, provided, however, that the Board shall not have the power to acquire any interest in real property other than (I) temporarily to hold real property donated to it and (II) to acquire leased office space;

(b) To promulgate rules and regulations as are necessary or expedient for the conduct of its affairs and its meetings and of meetings of any committees and generally for the administration of this article, provided, however, that such rules and regulations shall give the public an opportunity to comment on the general policies of the Board and upon specific grant proposals before the Board;

(c) To cause to be published and distributed an annual report, including a financial report, to the citizens, the Governor and the General Assembly of Colorado, which will set out the Board's progress in administering the funds appropriated to it, and the Board's objectives and its budget for the forthcoming year, and to consult with the General Assembly from time to time concerning its objectives and its budget;

(d) To administer the distribution of grants pursuant to Sections 1 (1) (c), 1 (1) (d), 5 (1) (a) (III), and 5 (1) (a) (IV) of this article, with the expense of administering said grants to be defrayed from the funds made available to the program elements of said sections;

(e) Commencing July 1, 1993, to determine what portions, if any, of moneys allocated to the Trust Fund should be invested in an interest-bearing Trust Fund account by the Treasurer of the State of Colorado, to remain in the Trust Fund and available for expenditure in future years;

(f) To employ such staff and to contract for such office space and acquire such equipment and supplies and enter into such other contracts as it may consider necessary from time to time to accomplish its purposes, and to pay the cost thereof from the funds appropriated to the Board under this article, provided, however, that to the extent it is reasonably feasible to do so the Board shall (I) contract with the Colorado Department of Natural Resources or other state agency for necessary administrative support and (II) endeavor to keep the level of administrative expense as low as may be practicable in comparison with its expenditures for the purposes set forth in Section 1 of this article, and the Board may contract with the State Personnel Board or any successor thereof for personnel services.

(3) The Board shall be a political subdivision of the state, and shall have all the duties, privileges, immunities, rights, liabilities and disabilities of a political subdivision of the state, provided, however, that its organization, powers, revenues and expenses shall not be affected by any order or resolution of the general assembly, except as provided in this constitution. It shall not be an agency of state government, nor shall it be subject to administrative direction by any department, commission, board, bureau or agency of the state, except to the extent provided in this constitution. The Board shall be subject to annual audit by the state auditor, whose report shall be a public document. The Board shall adopt rules permitting public access to its meetings and records which are no less restrictive than state laws applicable to state agencies, as such laws may be amended from time to time. The Board members, officers and directors of the Board shall have no personal liability for any actions or refusal to act by the Board as long as such action or refusal to act did not involve willful or intentional malfeasance or gross negligence.

Section 7. No Effect on Colorado Water
Nothing in this article shall affect in any way whatsoever any of the provisions under Article XVI of the State Constitution of Colorado, including those provisions related to water, nor any of the statutory provisions related to the appropriation of water in Colorado.

Section 8. No Substitution Allowed.
The people intend that the allocation of lottery funds required by this article of the constitution be in addition to and not a substitute for funds otherwise appropriated from the General Assembly to the Colorado Department of Natural Resources and its divisions.

Section 9. Eminent Domain.
No moneys received by any state agency pursuant to this article shall be used to acquire real property by condemnation through the power of eminent domain.

Section 10. Payment in Lieu of Taxes.
Any acquisitions of real property made by a state agency pursuant to this article shall be subject to payments in lieu of taxes to counties in which said acquisitions are made. Such payments shall be made from moneys made available by the Trust Fund, and shall not exceed the rate of taxation for comparable property classifications.

Article XXVIII: Campaign and Political Finance

Section 1. Purpose and findings

The people of the state of Colorado hereby find and declare that large campaign contributions to political candidates create the potential for corruption and the appearance of corruption; that large campaign contributions made to influence election outcomes allow wealthy individuals, corporations, and special interest groups to exercise a disproportionate level of influence over the political process; that the rising costs of campaigning for political office prevent qualified citizens from running for political office; that because of the use of early voting in Colorado timely notice of independent expenditures is essential for informing the electorate; that in recent years the advent of significant spending on electioneering communications, as defined herein, has frustrated the purpose of existing campaign finance requirements; that independent research has demonstrated that the vast majority of televised electioneering communications goes beyond issue discussion to express electoral advocacy; that political contributions from corporate treasuries are not an indication of popular support for the corporation's political ideas and can unfairly influence the outcome of Colorado elections; and that the interests of the public are best served by limiting campaign contributions, encouraging voluntary campaign spending limits, providing for full and timely disclosure of campaign contributions, independent expenditures, and funding of electioneering communications, and strong enforcement of campaign finance requirements.

Section 2. Definitions.

For the purpose of this Article and any statutory provisions pertaining to campaign finance, including provisions pertaining to disclosure:

(1) Appropriate officer" means the individual with whom a candidate, candidate committee, political committee, small donor committee, or issue committee must file pursuant to section 1-45-109 (1), C.R.S., or any successor section.

(2) "Candidate" means any person who seeks nomination or election to any state or local public office that is to be voted on in this state at any primary election, general election, school district election, special district election, or municipal election. "Candidate" also includes a judge or justice of any court of record who seeks to be retained in office pursuant to the provisions of section 25 of article VI. A person is a candidate for election if the person has publicly announced an intention to seek election to public office or retention of a judicial office and thereafter has received a contribution or made an expenditure in support of the candidacy. A person remains a candidate for purposes of this Article so long as the candidate maintains a registered candidate committee. A person who maintains a candidate committee after an election cycle, but who has not publicly announced an intention to seek election to public office in the next or any subsequent election cycle, is a candidate for purposes of this article.

(3) "Candidate committee" means a person, including the candidate, or persons with the common purpose of receiving contributions or making expenditures under the authority of a candidate. A contribution to a candidate shall be deemed a contribution to the candidate's candidate committee. A candidate shall have only one candidate committee. A candidate committee shall be considered open and active until affirmatively closed by the candidate or by action of the secretary of state.

(4) "Conduit" means a person who transmits contributions from more than one person, directly to a candidate committee. "Conduit" does not include the contributor's immediate family members, the candidate or campaign treasurer of the candidate committee receiving the contribution, a volunteer fund raiser hosting an event for a candidate committee, or a professional fund raiser if the fund raiser is compensated at the usual and customary rate.

(5) (a) "Contribution" means:

(I) The payment, loan, pledge, gift, or advance of money, or guarantee of a loan, made to any candidate committee, issue committee, political committee, small donor committee, or political party;

(II) Any payment made to a third party for the benefit of any candidate committee, issue committee, political committee, small donor committee, or political party;

(III) The fair market value of any gift or loan of property made to any candidate committee, issue committee, political committee, small donor committee or political party;

(IV) Anything of value given, directly or indirectly, to a candidate for the purpose of promoting the candidate's nomination, retention, recall, or election.

(b) "Contribution" does not include services provided without compensation by individuals volunteering their time on behalf of a candidate, candidate committee, political committee, small donor committee, issue committee, or political party; a transfer by a membership organization of a portion of a member's dues to a small donor committee or political committee sponsored by such membership organization; or payments by a corporation or labor organization for the costs of establishing, administering, and soliciting funds from its own employees or members for a political committee or small donor committee.

(6) "Election cycle" means either:

(a) The period of time beginning thirty-one days following a general election for the particular office and ending thirty days following the next general election for that office;

(b) The period of time beginning thirty-one days following a general election for the particular office and ending thirty days following the special legislative election for that office; or

(c) The period of time beginning thirty-one days following the special legislative election for the particular office and ending thirty days following the next general election for that office.

(7) (a) "Electioneering communication" means any communication broadcasted by television or radio, printed in a newspaper or on a billboard, directly mailed or delivered by hand to personal residences or otherwise distributed that:

(I) Unambiguously refers to any candidate; and
(II) Is broadcasted, printed, mailed, delivered, or distributed within thirty days before a primary election or sixty days before a general election; and
(III) Is broadcasted to, printed in a newspaper distributed to, mailed to, delivered by hand to, or otherwise distributed to an audience that includes members of the electorate for such public office.

(b) "Electioneering communication" does not include:

(I) Any news Articles, editorial endorsements, opinion or commentary writings, or letters to the editor printed in a newspaper, magazine or other periodical not owned or controlled by a candidate or political party;
(II) Any editorial endorsements or opinions aired by a broadcast facility not owned or controlled by a candidate or political party;
(III) Any communication by persons made in the regular course and scope of their business or any communication made by a membership organization solely to members of such organization and their families;
(IV) Any communication that refers to any candidate only as part of the popular name of a bill or statute.

(8) (a) "Expenditure" means any purchase, payment, distribution, loan, advance, deposit, or gift of money by any person for the purpose of expressly advocating the election or defeat of a candidate or supporting or opposing a ballot issue or ballot question. An expenditure is made when the actual spending occurs or when there is a contractual agreement requiring such spending and the amount is determined.
(b) "Expenditure" does not include:

(I) Any news Articles, editorial endorsements, opinion or commentary writings, or letters to the editor printed in a newspaper, magazine or other periodical not owned or controlled by a candidate or political party;

(II) Any editorial endorsements or opinions aired by a broadcast facility not owned or controlled by a candidate or political party;

(III) Spending by persons, other than political parties, political committees and small donor committees, in the regular course and scope of their business or payments by a membership organization for any communication solely to members and their families;

(IV) Any transfer by a membership organization of a portion of a member's dues to a small donor committee or political committee sponsored by such membership organization; or payments made by a corporation or labor organization for the costs of establishing, administering, or soliciting funds from its own employees or members for a political committee or small donor committee.

(9) "Independent expenditure" means an expenditure that is not controlled by or coordinated with any candidate or agent of such candidate. Expenditures that are controlled by or coordinated with a candidate or candidate's agent are deemed to be both contributions by the maker of the expenditures, and expenditures by the candidate committee.

(10) (a) "Issue committee" means any person, other than a natural person, or any group of two or more persons, including natural persons:

(I) That has a major purpose of supporting or opposing any ballot issue or ballot question; or

(II) That has accepted or made contributions or expenditures in excess of two hundred dollars to support or oppose any ballot issue or ballot question.

(b) "Issue committee" does not include political parties, political committees, small donor committees, or candidate committees as otherwise defined in this section.
(c) An issue committee shall be considered open and active until affirmatively closed by such committee or by action of the appropriate authority.

(11) "Person" means any natural person, partnership, committee, association, corporation, labor organization, political party, or other organization or group of persons.

(12) (a) "Political committee" means any person, other than a natural person, or any group of two or more persons, including natural persons that have accepted or made contributions or expenditures in excess of $200 to support or oppose the nomination or election of one or more candidates.
(b) "Political committee" does not include political parties, issue committees, or candidate committees as otherwise defined in this section.
(c) For the purposes of this Article, the following are treated as a single political committee:

(I) All political committees established, financed, maintained, or controlled by a single corporation or its subsidiaries;
(II) All political committees established, financed, maintained, or controlled by a single labor organization; except that, any political committee established, financed, maintained, or controlled by a local unit of the labor organization which has the authority to make a decision independently of the state and national units as to which candidates to support or oppose shall be deemed separate from the political committee of the state and national unit;
(III) All political committees established, financed, maintained, or controlled by the same political party;
(IV) All political committees established, financed, maintained, or controlled by substantially the same group of persons.

(13) "Political party" means any group of registered electors who, by petition or assembly, nominate candidates for the official general election ballot. "Political party" includes affiliated party organizations at the state, county, and election district levels, and all such affiliates are considered to be a single entity for the purposes of this Article, except as otherwise provided in section 7.

(14) (a) "Small donor committee" means any political committee that has accepted contributions only from natural persons who each contributed no more than fifty dollars in the aggregate per year. For purposes of this section, dues transferred by a membership organization to a small donor committee sponsored by such organization shall be treated as pro-rata contributions from individual members.
(b) "Small donor committee" does not include political parties, political committees, issue committees, or candidate committees as otherwise defined in this section.
(c) For the purposes of this Article, the following are treated as a single small donor committee:

(I) All small donor committees established, financed, maintained, or controlled by a single corporation or its subsidiaries;
(II) All small donor committees established, financed, maintained, or controlled by a single labor organization; except that, any small donor committee established, financed, maintained, or controlled by a local unit of the labor organization which has the authority to make a decision independently of the state and national units as to which candidates to support or oppose shall be deemed separate from the small donor committee of the state and national unit;
(III) All small donor committees established, financed, maintained, or controlled by the same political party;
(IV) All small donor committees established, financed, maintained, or controlled by substantially the same group of persons.

(15) "Unexpended campaign contributions" means the balance of funds on hand in any candidate committee at the end of an election cycle, less the amount of all unpaid monetary obligations incurred prior to the election in furtherance of such candidacy.

Section 3. Contribution limits.

(1) Except as described in subsections (2), (3), and (4) of this section, no person, including a political committee, shall make to a candidate committee, and no candidate committee shall accept from any one person, aggregate contributions for a primary or a general election in excess of the following amounts:

(a) Five hundred dollars to any one:

(I) Governor candidate committee for the primary election, and governor and lieutenant governor candidate committee, as joint candidates under 1-1-104, C.R.S., or any successor section, for the general election;
(II) Secretary of state, state treasurer, or attorney general candidate committee; and

(b) Two hundred dollars to any one state senate, state house of representatives, state board of education, regent of the university of Colorado, or district attorney candidate committee.

(2) No small donor committee shall make to a candidate committee, and no candidate committee shall accept from any one small donor committee, aggregate contributions for a primary or a general election in excess of the following amounts:

(a) Five thousand dollars to any one:

(I) Governor candidate committee for the primary election, and governor and lieutenant governor candidate committee, as joint candidates under 1-1-104, C.R.S., or any successor section, for the general election;
(II) Secretary of state, state treasurer, or attorney general

candidate committee; and

(b) Two thousand dollars to any one state senate, state house of representatives, state board of education, regent of the university of Colorado, or district attorney candidate committee.

(3) (a) No political party shall accept aggregate contributions from any person, other than a small donor committee as described in paragraph (b) of this subsection (3), that exceed three thousand dollars per year at the state, county, district, and local level combined, and of such amount no more than twenty-five hundred dollars per year at the state level;
(b) No political party shall accept aggregate contributions from any small donor committee that exceed fifteen thousand dollars per year at the state, county, district, and local level combined, and of such amount no more than twelve thousand, five hundred dollars at the state level;
(c) No political party shall accept contributions that are intended, or in any way designated, to be passed through the party to a specific candidate's candidate committee;
(d) In the applicable election cycle, no political party shall contribute to any candidate committee more than twenty percent of the applicable spending limit set forth in section 4 of this Article.
(e) Any unexpended campaign contributions retained by a candidate committee for use in a subsequent election cycle shall be counted and reported as contributions from a political party in any subsequent election for purposes of paragraph (d) of this subsection (3);

(4) (a) It shall be unlawful for a corporation or labor organization to make contributions to a candidate committee or a political party, and to make expenditures expressly advocating the election or defeat of a candidate; except that a corporation or labor organization may establish a political committee or small donor committee which may accept contributions or dues from employees, officeholders, shareholders, or members.
(b) The prohibition contained in paragraph (a) of this subsection

(4) shall not apply to a corporation that:

(I) Is formed for the purpose of promoting political ideas and cannot engage in business activities; and
(II) Has no shareholders or other persons with a claim on its assets or income; and
(III) Was not established by and does not accept contributions from business corporations or labor organizations.

(5) No political committee shall accept aggregate contributions or pro-rata dues from any person in excess of five hundred dollars per house of representatives election cycle.
(6) No candidate's candidate committee shall accept contributions from, or make contributions to, another candidate committee, including any candidate committee, or equivalent entity, established under federal law.
(7) No person shall act as a conduit for a contribution to a candidate committee.
(8) Notwithstanding any other section of this Article to the contrary, a candidate's candidate committee may receive a loan from a financial institution organized under state or federal law if the loan bears the usual and customary interest rate, is made on a basis that assures repayment, is evidenced by a written instrument, and is subject to a due date or amortization schedule. The contribution limits described in this section shall not apply to a loan as described in this subsection (8).
(9) All contributions received by a candidate committee, issue committee, political committee, small donor committee, or political party shall be deposited in a financial institution in a separate account whose title shall include the name of the committee or political party. All records pertaining to such accounts shall be maintained by the committee or political party for one-hundred eighty days following any general election in which the committee or party received contributions unless a complaint is filed, in which case they shall be maintained until final disposition of the complaint and any consequent litigation. Such records shall be subject to inspection at any hearing held pursuant to this Article.

(10) No candidate committee, political committee, small donor committee, issue committee, or political party shall accept a contribution, or make an expenditure, in currency or coin exceeding one hundred dollars.

(11) No person shall make a contribution to a candidate committee, issue committee, political committee, small donor committee, or political party with the expectation that some or all of the amounts of such contribution will be reimbursed by another person. No person shall be reimbursed for a contribution made to any candidate committee, issue committee, political committee, small donor committee, or political party, nor shall any person make such reimbursement except as provided in subsection (8) of this section.

(12) No candidate committee, political committee, small donor committee, or political party shall knowingly accept contributions from:

(a) Any natural person who is not a citizen of the United States;
(b) A foreign government; or
(c) Any foreign corporation that does not have the authority to transact business in this state pursuant to Article 115 of title 7, C.R.S., or any successor section.

(13) Each limit on contributions described in subsections (1), (2), (3) (a), (3) (b) and (5) of this section, and subsection (14) of section 2, shall be adjusted by an amount based upon the percentage change over a four year period in the United States bureau of labor statistics consumer price index for Denver-Boulder-Greeley, all items, all consumers, or its successor index, rounded to the nearest lowest twenty-five dollars. The first adjustment shall be done in the first quarter of 2007 and then every four years thereafter. The secretary of state shall calculate such an adjustment in each limit and specify the limits in rules promulgated in accordance with article 4 of title 24, C.R.S., or any successor section.

Section 4. Voluntary campaign spending limits.

(1) Candidates may certify to the secretary of state that the candidate's candidate committee shall not exceed the following spending limits for the applicable election cycle:

(a) Two and one-half million dollars combined for a candidate for governor and governor and lieutenant governor as joint candidates under 1-1-104, C.R.S., or any successor section;
(b) Five hundred thousand dollars for a candidate for secretary of state, attorney general, or treasurer;
(c) Ninety thousand dollars for a candidate for the state senate;
(d) Sixty-five thousand dollars for a candidate for the state house of representatives, state board of education, regent of the university of Colorado, or district attorney.

(2) Candidates accepting the campaign spending limits set forth above shall also agree that their personal contributions to their own campaign shall be counted as political party contributions and subject to the aggregate limit on such contributions set forth in section 3 of this article.
(3) Each candidate who chooses to accept the applicable voluntary spending limit shall file a statement to that effect with the secretary of state at the time that the candidate files a candidate affidavit as currently set forth in section 1-45-110(1), C.R.S., or any successor section. Acceptance of the applicable voluntary spending limit shall be irrevocable except as set forth in subsection (4) of this section and shall subject the candidate to the penalties set forth in section 10 of this Article for exceeding the limit.
(4) If a candidate accepts the applicable spending limit and another candidate for the same office refuses to accept the spending limit, the accepting candidate shall have ten days in which to withdraw acceptance. The accepting candidate shall have this option of withdrawing acceptance after each additional non-accepting candidate for the same office enters the race.
(5) The applicable contribution limits set forth in section 3 of this Article shall double for any candidate who has accepted the

applicable voluntary spending limit if:

(a) Another candidate in the race for the same office has not accepted the voluntary spending limit; and
(b) The non-accepting candidate has raised more than ten percent of the applicable voluntary spending limit.

(6) Only those candidates who have agreed to abide by the applicable voluntary spending limit may advertise their compliance. All other candidates are prohibited from advertising, or in any way implying, their acceptance of voluntary spending limits.

(7) Each spending limit described in subsection (1) of this section shall be adjusted by an amount based upon the percentage change over a four year period in the united states bureau of labor statistics consumer price index for Denver-Boulder-Greeley, all items, all consumers, or its successor index, rounded to the nearest lowest twenty-five dollars. The first adjustment shall be done in the first quarter of 2007 and then every four years thereafter. The secretary of state shall calculate such an adjustment in each limit and specify the limits in rules promulgated in accordance with Article 4 of title 24, C.R.S., or any successor section.

Section 5. Independent expenditures.

(1) Any person making an independent expenditure in excess of one thousand dollars per calendar year shall deliver notice in writing to the secretary of state of such independent expenditure, as well as the amount of such expenditure, and a detailed description of the use of such independent expenditure. The notice shall specifically state the name of the candidate whom the independent expenditure is intended to support or oppose. Each independent expenditure in excess of one-thousand dollars shall require the delivery of a new notice. Any person making an independent expenditure within thirty days of a primary or general election shall deliver such notice within forty-eight hours after obligating funds for such expenditure.

(2) Any person making an independent expenditure in excess of one thousand dollars shall disclose, in the communication produced by the expenditure, the name of the person making the expenditure and the specific statement that the advertisement of material is not authorized by any candidate. Such disclosure shall be prominently featured in the communication.

(3) Expenditures by any person on behalf of a candidate for public office that are coordinated with or controlled by the candidate or the candidate's agent, or political party shall be considered a contribution to the candidate's candidate committee, or the political party, respectively. 7

(4) This section 5 applies only to independent expenditures made for the purpose of expressly advocating the defeat or election of any candidate.

Section 6. Electioneering communications.

(1) Any person who expends one thousand dollars or more per calendar year on electioneering communications shall submit reports to the secretary of state in accordance with the schedule currently set forth in 1-45-108 (2), C.R.S., or any successor section. Such reports shall include spending on such electioneering communications, and the name, and address, of any person that contributes more than two hundred and fifty dollars per year to such person described in this section for an electioneering communication. In the case where the person is a natural person, such reports shall also include the occupation and employer of such natural person. The last such report shall be filed thirty days after the applicable election.

(2) Notwithstanding any section to the contrary, it shall be unlawful for a corporation or labor organization to provide funding for an electioneering communication; except that any political committee or small donor committee established by such corporation or labor organization may provide funding for an electioneering communication.

Section 7. Disclosure.
The disclosure requirements relevant to candidate committees, political committees, issue committees, and political parties, that are currently set forth in section 1-45-108, C.R.S., or any successor section, shall be extended to include small donor committees. The disclosure requirements of section 1-45-108, C.R.S., or any successor section, shall be extended to require disclosure of the occupation and employer of each person who has made a contribution of one hundred dollars or more to a candidate committee, political committee, issue committee, or political party. For purposes of this section and 1-45-108, C.R.S., or any successor section, a political party shall be treated as separate entities at the state, county, district, and local levels.
Section 8. Filing - where to file - timeliness.
The secretary of state shall promulgate rules relating to filing in accordance with article 4 of title 24, C.R.S., or any successor section. The rules promulgated pursuant to this section shall extend section 1- 45-109, C.R.S., or any successor section to apply to small donor committees.

Section 9. Duties of the secretary of state - enforcement.

(1) The secretary of state shall:

(a) Prepare forms and instructions to assist candidates and the public in complying with the reporting requirements of this article and make such forms and instructions available to the public, municipal clerks, and county clerk and recorders free of charge;
(b) Promulgate such rules, in accordance with Article 4 of title 24, C.R.S., or any successor section, as may be necessary to administer and enforce any provision of this Article;
(c) Prepare forms for candidates to declare their voluntary acceptance of the campaign spending limits set forth in section 4 of this Article. Such forms shall include an acknowledgment that the candidate voluntarily accepts the applicable spending limit and that the candidate swears to abide by those spending limits. These forms shall be signed by the candidate under oath,

notarized, filed with the secretary of state, and available to the public upon request;

(d) Maintain a filing and indexing system consistent with the purposes of this Article;

(e) Make the reports and statements filed with the secretary of state's office available immediately for public inspection and copying. The secretary of state may charge a reasonable fee for providing copies of reports. No information copied from such reports shall be sold or used by any person for the purpose of soliciting contributions or for any commercial purpose;

(f) Refer any complaints filed against any candidate for the office of secretary of state to the attorney general. Any administrative law judge employed pursuant to this section shall be appointed pursuant to part 10 of Article 30 of title 24, C.R.S., or any successor section. Any hearing conducted by an administrative law judge employed pursuant to subsection (2) of this section shall be conducted in accordance with the provisions of section 24-4-105, C.R.S., or any successor section.

(2) (a) Any person who believes that a violation of section 3, section 4, section 5, section 6, section 7, or section 9 (1) (e), of this Article, or of sections 1-45-108, 1-45-114, 1-45-115, or 1-45-117 C.R.S., or any successor sections, has occurred may file a written complaint with the secretary of state no later than one hundred eighty days after the date of the alleged violation. The secretary of state shall refer the complaint to an administrative law judge within three days of the filing of the complaint. The administrative law judge shall hold a hearing within fifteen days of the referral of the complaint, and shall render a decision within fifteen days of the hearing. The defendant shall be granted an extension of up to thirty days upon defendant's motion, or longer upon a showing of good cause. If the administrative law judge determines that such violation has occurred, such decision shall include any appropriate order, sanction, or relief authorized by this Article. The decision of the administrative law judge shall be final and subject to review by the court of appeals, pursuant to section 24-4-106 (11), C.R.S., or any successor section. The secretary of state and the administrative law judge are not necessary parties to the review. The decision maybe enforced by the secretary of state, or, if the secretary of state does not file an enforcement action within thirty days of the decision, in a private cause of action by the person filing the complaint. Any private action brought under this section shall be brought within one year of the date of the violation in state district court. The prevailing party in a private enforcement action shall be entitled to reasonable attorneys fees and costs.

(b) The attorney general shall investigate complaints made against any candidate for the office of secretary of state using the same procedures set forth in paragraph (a) of this subsection

(2). Complainant shall have the same private right of action as under paragraph (a) of this subsection (2).

(c) A subpoena issued by an administrative law judge requiring the production of documents by an issue committee shall be limited to documents pertaining to contributions to, or expenditures from, the committee's separate account established pursuant to section 3(9) of this Article to support or oppose a ballot issue or ballot question. A subpoena shall not be limited in this manner where such issue committee fails to form a separate account through which a ballot issue or ballot question is supported or opposed.

Section 10. Sanctions.

(1) Any person who violates any provision of this Article relating to contribution or voluntary spending limits shall be subject to a civil penalty of at least double and up to five times the amount contributed, received, or spent in violation of the applicable provision of this Article. Candidates shall be personally liable for penalties imposed upon the candidate's committee.

(2) (a) The appropriate officer shall impose a penalty of fifty dollars per day for each day that a statement or other information required to be filed pursuant to section 5, section 6, or section 7 of this Article, or sections 1-45-108, 1-45-109 or 1-45-110, C.R.S., or any successor sections, is not filed by the close of business on the day due. Upon imposition of a penalty pursuant to this subsection (2), the appropriate officer shall send the person upon whom the penalty is being imposed proper notification by certified mail of the imposition of the penalty. If an electronic mail address is on file with the secretary of state, the secretary of state shall also provide such notification by electronic mail. Revenues collected from fees and penalties assessed by the secretary of state or revenues collected in the form of payment of the secretary of state's attorney fees and costs pursuant to this Article shall be deposited in the department of state cash fund created in section 24-21-104 (3), C.R.S., or any successor section.

(b) (I) Any person required to file a report with the secretary of state and upon whom a penalty has been imposed pursuant to this subsection (2) may appeal such penalty by filing a written appeal with the secretary of state no later than thirty days after the date on which notification of the imposition of the penalty was mailed to such person's last known address in accordance with paragraph (a) of this subsection (2). Except as provided in paragraph (c) of this subsection (2), the secretary shall refer the appeal to an administrative law judge. Any hearing conducted by an administrative law judge pursuant to this subsection (2) shall be conducted in accordance with the provisions of section 24-4-105, C.R.S., or any successor section. The administrative law judge shall set aside or reduce the penalty upon a showing of good cause, and the person filing the appeal shall bear the burden of proof. The decision of the administrative law judge shall be final and subject to review by the court of appeals pursuant to section 24-4-106 (11), C.R.S., or any successor section.

(II) If the administrative law judge finds that the filing of an appeal brought pursuant to subparagraph (I) of this paragraph (b) was frivolous, groundless, or vexatious, the administrative law judge shall order the person filing the appeal to pay reasonable attorney fees and costs of the secretary of state in connection with such proceeding.

(c) Upon receipt by the secretary of state of an appeal pursuant to paragraph (b) of this subsection (2), the secretary shall set aside or reduce the penalty upon a showing of good cause.

(d) Any unpaid debt owing to the state resulting from a penalty imposed pursuant to this subsection (2) shall be collected by the state in accordance with the requirements of section 24-30-202.4, C.R.S., or any successor section.

(3) Failure to comply with the provisions of this article shall have no effect on the validity of any election.

Section 11. Conflicting provisions declared inapplicable. Any provisions in the statutes of this state in conflict or inconsistent with this article are hereby declared to be inapplicable to the matters covered and provided for in this Article.

Section 12. Repeal of conflicting statutory provisions.
Sections 1-45-103, 1-45-105.3, 1-45-107, 1-45-111, and 1-45-113 are repealed.

Section 13. Applicability and effective date.
The provisions of this article shall take effect on December 6, 2002 and be applicable for all elections thereafter. Legislation may be enacted to facilitate its operations, but in no way limiting or restricting the provisions of this Article or the powers herein granted.

Section 14. Severability.
If any provision of this Article or the application thereof to any person or circumstances is held invalid, such invalidity shall not affect other provisions or applications of the Article which can be given effect without the invalid provision or application, and to this end the provisions of this Article are declared to be severable.

Article XXIX: Ethics in Government

Section 1. Purposes and Findings.

(1) The people of the state of Colorado hereby find and declare that:

(a) The conduct of public officers, members of the general assembly, local government officials, and government employees must hold the respect and confidence of the people;
(b) They shall carry out their duties for the benefit of the people of the state;
(c) They shall, therefore, avoid conduct that is in violation of their public trust or that creates a justifiable impression among members of the public that such trust is being violated;
(d) Any effort to realize personal financial gain through public office other than compensation provided by law is a violation of that trust; and
(e) To ensure propriety and to preserve public confidence, they must have the benefit of specific standards to guide their conduct, and of a penalty mechanism to enforce those standards.

(2) The people of the state of Colorado also find and declare that there are certain costs associated with holding public office and that to ensure the integrity of the office, such costs of a reasonable and necessary nature should be born by the state or local government.

Section 2. Definitions.
As used in this article, unless the context otherwise requires:

(1) "Government employee" means any employee, including independent contractors, of the state executive branch, the state legislative branch, a state agency, a public institution of higher education, or any local government, except a member of the general assembly or a public officer.

(2) "Local government" means county or municipality.
(3) "Local government official" means an elected or appointed official of a local government but does not include an employee of a local government.
(4) "Person" means any individual, corporation, business trust, estate, trust, limited liability company, partnership, labor organization, association, political party, committee, or other legal entity.
(5) "Professional lobbyist" means any individual who engages himself or herself or is engaged by any other person for pay or for any consideration for lobbying. "Professional lobbyist" does not include any volunteer lobbyist, any state official or employee acting in his or her official capacity, except those designated as lobbyists as provided by law, any elected public official acting in his or her official capacity, or any individual who appears as counsel or advisor in an adjudicatory proceeding.
(6) "Public officer" means any elected officer, including all statewide elected officeholders, the head of any department of the executive branch, and elected and appointed members of state boards and commissions. "Public officer" does not include a member of the general assembly, a member of the judiciary, any local government official, or any member of a board, commission, council or committee who receives no compensation other than a per diem allowance or necessary and reasonable expenses.

Section 3. Gift ban.

(1) No public officer, member of the general assembly, local government official, or government employee shall accept or receive any money, forbearance, or forgiveness of indebtedness from any person, without such person receiving lawful consideration of equal or greater value in return from the public officer, member of the general assembly, local government official, or government employee who accepted or received the money, forbearance or forgiveness of indebtedness.
(2) No public officer, member of the general assembly, local government official, or government employee, either directly or

indirectly as the beneficiary of a gift or thing of value given to such person's spouse or dependent child, shall solicit, accept or receive any gift or other thing of value having either a fair market value or aggregate actual cost greater than fifty dollars ($50) in any calendar year, including but not limited to, gifts, loans, rewards, promises or negotiations of future employment, favors or services, honoraria, travel, entertainment, or special discounts, from a person, without the person receiving lawful consideration of equal or greater value in return from the public officer, member of the general assembly, local government official, or government employee who solicited, accepted or received the gift or other thing of value.

(3) The prohibitions in subsections (1) and (2) of this section do not apply if the gift or thing of value is:

(a) A campaign contribution as defined by law;

(b) An unsolicited item of trivial value less than fifty dollars ($50), such as a pen, calendar, plant, book, note pad or other similar item;

(c) An unsolicited token or award of appreciation in the form of a plaque, trophy, desk item, wall memento, or similar item;

(d) Unsolicited informational material, publications, or subscriptions related to the recipient's performance of official duties;

(e) Admission to, and the cost of food or beverages consumed at, a reception, meal or meeting by an organization before whom the recipient appears to speak or to answer questions as part of a scheduled program;

(f) Reasonable expenses paid by a nonprofit organization or other state or local government for attendance at a convention, fact-finding mission or trip, or other meeting if the person is scheduled to deliver a speech, make a presentation, participate on a panel, or represent the state or local government, provided that the nonprofit organization receives less than five percent (5%) of its funding from for-profit organizations or entities;

(g) Given by an individual who is a relative or personal friend of the recipient on a special occasion.

(h) A component of the compensation paid or other incentive given to the recipient in the normal course of employment.

(4) Notwithstanding any provisions of this section to the contrary, and excepting campaign contributions as defined by law, no professional lobbyist, personally or on behalf of any other person or entity, shall knowingly offer, give, or arrange to give, to any public officer, member of the general assembly, local government official, or government employee, or to a member of such person's immediate family, any gift or thing of value, of any kind or nature, nor knowingly pay for any meal, beverage, or other item to be consumed by such public officer, member of the general assembly, local government official or government employee, whether or not such gift or meal, beverage or other item to be consumed is offered, given or paid for in the course of such lobbyist's business or in connection with a personal or social event; provided, however, that a professional lobbyist shall not be prohibited from offering or giving to a public officer, member of the general assembly, local government official or government employee who is a member of his or her immediate family any such gift, thing of value, meal, beverage or other item.

(5) The general assembly shall make any conforming amendments to the reporting and disclosure requirements for public officers, members of the general assembly and professional lobbyists, as provided by law, to comply with the requirements set forth in this section.

(6) The fifty-dollar ($50) limit set forth in subsection (2) of this section shall be adjusted by an amount based upon the percentage change over a four-year period in the United States bureau of labor statistics consumer price index for Denver-Boulder-Greeley, all items, all consumers, or its successor index, rounded to the nearest lowest dollar. The first adjustment shall be done in the first quarter of 2011 and then every four years thereafter.

Section 4. Restrictions on representation after leaving office.

No statewide elected officeholder or member of the general assembly shall personally represent another person or entity for compensation before any other statewide elected officeholder or member of the general assembly, for a period of two years following vacation of office. Further restrictions on public officers or members of the general assembly and similar restrictions on other public officers, local government officials or government employees may be established by law.

Section 5. Independent ethics commission.

(1) There is hereby created an independent ethics commission to be composed of five members. The purpose of the independent ethics commission shall be to hear complaints, issue findings, and assess penalties, and also to issue advisory opinions, on ethics issues arising under this article and under any other standards of conduct and reporting requirements as provided by law. The independent ethics commission shall have authority to adopt such reasonable rules as may be necessary for the purpose of administering and enforcing the provisions of this article and any other standards of conduct and reporting requirements as provided by law. The general assembly shall appropriate reasonable and necessary funds to cover staff and administrative expenses to allow the independent ethics commission to carry out its duties pursuant to this article. Members of the commission shall receive no compensation for their services on the commission.

(2) (a) Members of the independent ethics commission shall be appointed in the following manner and order:

(I) One member shall be appointed by the Colorado senate;
(II) One member shall be appointed by the Colorado house of representatives;

(III) One member shall be appointed by the governor of the state of Colorado;
(IV) One member shall be appointed by the chief justice of the Colorado supreme court; and
(V) One member shall be either a local government official or a local government employee appointed by the affirmative vote of at least three of the four members appointed pursuant to subparagraphs (I) to (IV) of this paragraph (a).

(b) No more than two members shall be affiliated with the same political party.
(c) Each of the five members shall be registered Colorado voters and shall have been continuously registered with the same political party, or continuously unaffiliated with any political party, for at least two years prior to appointment to the commission.
(d) Members of the independent ethics commission shall be appointed to terms of four years; except that, the first member appointed by the Colorado senate and the first member appointed by the governor of the state of Colorado shall initially serve two year terms to achieve staggered ending dates.
(e) If a member is appointed to fill an unexpired term, that member's term shall end at the same time as the term of the person being replaced.
(f) Each member shall continue to serve until a successor has been appointed, except that if a member is unable or unwilling to continue to serve until a successor has been appointed, the original appointing authority as described in this subsection shall fill the vacancy promptly.

(3) (a) Any person may file a written complaint with the independent ethics commission asking whether a public officer, member of the general assembly, local government official, or government employee has failed to comply with this article or any other standards of conduct or reporting requirements as provided by law within the preceding twelve months.

(b) The commission may dismiss frivolous complaints without conducting a public hearing. Complaints dismissed as frivolous shall be maintained confidential by the commission.
(c) The commission shall conduct an investigation, hold a public hearing, and render findings on each non-frivolous complaint pursuant to written rules adopted by the commission.
(d) The commission may assess penalties for violations as prescribed by this article and provided by law.
(e) There is hereby established a presumption that the findings shall be based on a preponderance of evidence unless the commission determines that the circumstances warrant a heightened standard.

(4) Members of the independent ethics commission shall have the power to subpoena documents and to subpoena witnesses to make statements and produce documents.
(5) Any public officer, member of the general assembly, local government official, or government employee may submit a written request to the independent ethics commission for an advisory opinion on whether any conduct by that person would constitute a violation of this article, or any other standards of conduct or reporting requirements as provided by law. The commission shall render an advisory opinion pursuant to written rules adopted by the commission.

Section 6. Penalty.
Any public officer, member of the general assembly, local government official or government employee who breaches the public trust for private gain and any person or entity inducing such breach shall be liable to the state or local jurisdiction for double the amount of the financial equivalent of any benefits obtained by such actions. The manner of recovery and additional penalties may be provided by law.

Section 7. Counties and Municipalities.
Any county or municipality may adopt ordinances or charter provisions with respect to ethics matters that are more stringent than any of the provisions contained in this article. The requirements of this article shall not apply to home rule counties or home rule municipalities that have adopted charters, ordinances, or resolutions that address the matters covered by this article.

Section 8. Conflicting provisions declared inapplicable.
Any provisions in the statutes of this state in conflict or inconsistent with this article are hereby declared to be preempted by this article and inapplicable to the matters covered by and provided for in this article.

Section 9. Legislation to facilitate article.
Legislation may be enacted to facilitate the operation of this article, but in no way shall such legislation limit or restrict the provisions of this article or the powers herein granted.

Schedule

Preamble

That no inconvenience may arise by reason of the change in the form of government, it is hereby ordained and declared:

Section 1. All Laws Remain Till Repealed
That all laws in force at the adoption of this constitution shall, so far as not inconsistent therewith, remain of the same force as if this constitution had not been adopted, until they expire by their own limitation or are altered or repealed by the general assembly; and all rights, actions, prosecutions, claims and contracts of the territory of Colorado, counties, individuals or bodies corporate (not inconsistent therewith) shall continue as if the form of government had not been changed and this constitution adopted.

Section 2. Contracts -Recognizances -Indictments
That all recognizances, obligations and all other instruments entered into or executed before the admission of the state, to the territory of Colorado, or to any county, school district or other municipality therein, or any officer thereof, and all fines, taxes, penalties and forfeitures due or owing to the territory of Colorado, or any such county, school district or municipality, or officer; and all writs, prosecutions, actions and causes of action, except as herein otherwise provided, shall continue and remain unaffected by the change of the form of government. All indictments which shall have been found, or may hereafter be found, and all informations which shall have been filed, or may hereafter be filed, for any crime or offense committed before this constitution takes effect, may be proceeded upon as if no change had taken place, except as otherwise provided in the constitution.

Section 3. Territorial Property Vests in State

That all property, real and personal, and all moneys, credits, claims and choses in action, belonging to the territory of Colorado at the adoption of this constitution, shall be vested in and become the property of the state of Colorado.

Section 4. Duty of General Assembly

The general assembly shall pass all laws necessary to carry into effect the provisions of this constitution.

Section 5. Supreme and District Courts -Transition

Whenever any two of the judges of the supreme court of the state elected or appointed under the provisions of this constitution shall have qualified in their office, the causes theretofore pending in the supreme court of the territory, and the papers, records and proceedings of said court, and the seal and other property pertaining thereto, shall pass into the jurisdiction and possession of the supreme court of the state; and until so superseded the supreme court of the territory and the judges thereof shall continue with like powers and jurisdiction as if this constitution had not been adopted. Whenever the judge of the district court of any district elected or appointed under the provisions of this constitution, shall have qualified in his office, the several causes theretofore pending in the district court of the territory, within any county in such district, and the records, papers and proceedings of said district court, and the seal and other property pertaining thereto shall pass into the jurisdiction and possession of the district court of the state, for such county, and until the district courts of the territory shall be superseded in manner aforesaid, the said district courts and the judges thereof shall continue with the same jurisdiction and powers to be exercised in the same judicial districts respectively as heretofore constituted under the laws of the territory.

Section 6. Judges -District Attorneys -Term Commence on Filing Oath

The terms of office of the several judges of the supreme and district courts and the district attorneys of the several judicial districts first elected under this constitution, shall commence from the day of filing their respective oaths of office in the office of the secretary of state.

Section 7. Seals of Supreme and District Courts

Until otherwise provided by law, the seals now in use in the supreme and district courts of this territory are hereby declared to be the seals of the supreme and district courts respectively of the state.

Section 8. Probate Court -County Court

Whenever this constitution shall go into effect, the books, records, papers and proceedings of the probate court in each county, and all causes and matters of administration pending therein, shall pass into the jurisdiction and possession of the county court of the same county, and the said county court shall proceed to final decree or judgment, order or other determination, in the said several matters and causes, as the said probate court might have done if this constitution had not been adopted. And until the election of the county judges provided for in this constitution, the probate judges shall act as judges of the county courts within their respective counties, and the seal of the probate court in each county shall be the seal of the county court therein until the said court shall have procured a proper seal.

Section 9. Terms Probate Court, Probate Judge, Apply to County Court, County Judge

The terms "Probate Court" or "Probate Judge," whenever occurring in the statutes of Colorado territory, shall, after the adoption of this constitution, be held to apply to the county court or county judge, and all laws specially applicable to the probate court in any county, shall be construed to apply to and be in force as to the county court in the same county, until repealed.

Section 10. County and Precinct Officers
All county and precinct officers, who may be in office at the time of the adoption of this constitution, shall hold their respective offices for the full time for which they may have been elected, and until such time as their successors may be elected and qualified in accordance with the provisions of this constitution, and the official bonds of all such officers shall continue in full force and effect as though this constitution had not been adopted.

Section 11. Vacancies in County Offices
All county offices that may become vacant during the year eighteen hundred and seventy- six by the expiration of the term of the persons elected to said offices, shall be filled at the general election on the first Tuesday in October in the year eighteen hundred and seventy -six, and, except county commissioners, the persons so elected shall hold their respective offices for the term of one year.

Section 12. Constitution Takes Effect on President's Proclamation
The provisions of this constitution shall be in force from the day on which the president of the United States shall issue his proclamation declaring the state of Colorado admitted into the Union; and the governor, secretary, treasurer, auditor and superintendent of public instruction of the territory of Colorado shall continue to discharge the duties of their respective offices after the admission of the state into the Union, until the qualification of the officers elected or appointed under the state government; and said officers, for the time they may serve, shall receive the same compensation as the state officers shall by law be paid for like services.

Section 13. First Election, Contest
In case of a contest of election between candidates, at the first general election under this constitution, for judges of the supreme, district or county courts, or district attorneys, the evidence shall be taken in the manner prescribed by territorial

law; and the testimony so taken shall be certified to the secretary of state, and said officer, together with the governor and attorney -general, shall review the testimony and determine who is entitled to the certificate of election.

Section 14. First Election -Canvass
The votes at the first general election under this constitution for the several officers provided for in this constitution who are to be elected at the first election shall be canvassed in the manner prescribed by the territorial law for canvassing votes for like officers. The votes cast for the judges of the supreme and district courts and district attorneys shall be canvassed by the county canvassing board in the manner prescribed by the territorial law for canvassing the votes for members of the general assembly; and the county clerk shall transmit the abstracts of votes to the secretary of the territory acting as secretary of state, under the same regulations as are prescribed by law for sending the abstracts of votes for territorial officers; and the aforesaid acting secretary of state, auditor, treasurer, or any two of them, in the presence of the governor, shall proceed to canvass the votes, under the regulations of sections thirty- five and thirty -six of chapter twenty- eight of the Revised Statutes of Colorado Territory.

Section 15. Senators Representatives -Districts
Senators and members of the house of representatives shall be chosen by the qualified electors of the several senatorial and representative districts as established in this constitution until such districts shall be changed by law; and thereafter by the qualified electors of the several districts as the same shall be established by law.

Section 16. Congressional Election - Canvass
The votes cast for representatives in congress at the first election held under this constitution shall be canvassed and the result determined in the manner provided by the laws of the territory for the canvass of votes for delegate in congress.

Section 17. General Assembly, First Session -Restrictions Removed

The provision of the constitution that no bill, except the general appropriation bill introduced in either house after the first twenty- five days of the session shall become a law, shall not apply to the first session of the general assembly; but no bill introduced in either house at the first session of the general assembly after the first fifty days thereof shall become a law.

Section 18. First General Election -Canvass

A copy of the abstracts of the votes cast at the first general election held under this constitution shall by the county clerks of the several counties be returned to the secretary of the territory immediately after the canvass of said votes in their several counties; and the secretary, auditor and treasurer of the territory, or any two of them, shall on the twenty- fifth day after the election, meet at the seat of government and proceed to canvass the votes cast for members of the general assembly and determine the result thereof.

Section 19. Presidential Electors, 1876

The general assembly shall, at their first session, immediately after the organization of the two houses and after the canvass of the votes for officers of the executive department, and before proceeding to other business, provide by act or joint resolution for the appointment by said general assembly of electors in the electoral college, and such joint resolution or the bill for such enactment may be passed without being printed or referred to any committee, or read on more than one day in either house, and shall take effect immediately after the concurrence of the two houses therein, and the approval of the governor thereto shall not be necessary.

Section 20. Presidential Electors After 1876

The general assembly shall provide that after the year eighteen hundred and seventy- six the electors of the electoral college shall be chosen by direct vote of the people.

Section 21. Expenses of Convention
The general assembly shall have power at their first session to provide for the payment of the expenses of this convention if any there be then remaining unpaid.

Section 22. Expenses of convention
Recognizances, bonds, payable to people continue. All recognizances, bail bonds, official bonds and other obligations or undertakings, which have been, or at any time before the admission of the state shall be made or entered into, and expressed to be payable to the people of the territory of Colorado, shall continue in full force notwithstanding the change in the form of government, and any breach thereof, whenever occurring, may after the admission of the state be prosecuted, in the name of the people of the state.

List of Delegates
Done in Convention at the city of Denver, Colorado, this fourteenth day of March in the year of our Lord one thousand eight hundred and seventy-six, and of the Independence of the United States the one hundredth.

In Witness Whereof, we have hereunto subscribed our names.

J. C. WILSON, President.
H. P. H. BROMWELL,
CASIMIRO BARELA,
GEORGE BOYLES,
W. E. BECK,
BYRON L. CARR,
WM. H. CUSHMAN,
WILLIAM M. CLARK,
A. D. COOPER,
HENRY R. CROSBY,
ROBERT DOUGLAS,
LEWIS C. ELLSWORTH,
CLARENCE P. ELDER,
F. J. EBERT,

WILLARD B. FELTON,
JESUS Ma GARCIA,
DANIEL HURD,
JOHN S. HOUGH,
LAFAYETTE HEAD,
WM. H. JAMES,
WM. R. KENNEDY,
WM. LEE,
ALVIN MARSH,
WM. H. MEYER,
S. J. PLUMB,
GEO. PEASE,
ROBERT A. QUILLIAN,
LEWIS C. ROCKWELL,
WILBUR F. STONE,
WILLIAM C. STOVER,
HENRY C. THATCHER,
AGAPITO VIGIL,
W. W. WEBSTER,
GEORGE G. WHITE,
EBENEZER T. WELLS,
P. P. WILCOX,
JOHN S. WHEELER,
J. W. WIDERFIELD,
ABRAM KNOX YOUNT.
Attest:
W. W. COULSON, Secretary.
HERBERT STANLEY, 1st Assistant Secretary.
H. A. TERPENNING, 2nd Assistant Secretary.

www.ingramcontent.com/pod-product-compliance
Lightning Source LLC
Chambersburg PA
CBHW052243220526
45471CB00001B/173